DR JANE MONCKTON SMITH is Professor of Public Protection at the University of Gloucestershire. She has an international reputation as an expert in her field and has published a number of academic books focused on homicide and criminal investigation. She has authored a new model for understanding and assessing risk of homicide in cases where there is domestic abuse. Her work is used widely in developing specialist practice for police and many other professionals. In addition to research she is also involved in homicide case work, reviewing cases for the Home Office, and advising police and review panels on complex and high-profile murders. She trains professionals in understanding risk escalation and homicide in cases of coercive control, stalking and domestic abuse.

@JMoncktonSmith

janems.blog

In Control

Dangerous Relationships and How They End in Murder

JANE MONCKTON SMITH

BLOOMSBURY PUBLISHING

LONDON · OXFORD · NEW YORK · NEW DELHI · SYDNEY

BLOOMSBURY PUBLISHING
Bloomsbury Publishing Plc
50 Bedford Square, London, WC1B 3DP, UK
29 Earlsfort Terrace, Dublin 2, Ireland

BLOOMSBURY, BLOOMSBURY PUBLISHING and the Diana logo
are trademarks of Bloomsbury Publishing Plc

First published in Great Britain 2021
This edition published 2022

A catalogue record for this book is available from the British Library

ISBN: HB: 978-1-5266-1321-9; TPB: 978-1-5266-1320-2; EBOOK: 978-1-5266-1319-6;
PB: 978-1-5266-1322-6

2 4 6 8 10 9 7 5 3 1

Typeset by Newgen KnowledgeWorks Pvt. Ltd., Chennai, India
Printed and bound in Great Britain by CPI Group (UK) Ltd, Croydon CR0 4YY

MIX
Paper from
responsible sources
FSC® C171272

To find out more about our authors and books visit
www.bloomsbury.com and sign up for our newsletters

I am so lucky to be able to hold my children. Not everyone has that privilege.

Minnie Aoife Westby
26th January 2018–21st January 2020

CONTENTS

PROLOGUE

The Homicide Timeline

Why won't she get in the ambulance?

It was eight o'clock in the evening and already dark when we arrived at the address, a Victorian building that had been split into flats. The flashing blue lights of the ambulance sparkled through the misty night rain, lighting up the open front door of the house and creating an uncomfortable eeriness in the quiet suburban street.

I was a newly qualified police officer, still in the first weeks of patrol duties, attending a 999 call with my supervising sergeant. We were coming towards the end of a long, hard shift and were due to finish around ten that evening. All we knew as we walked into that building was that there had been reports of an assault. I remember very clearly being warned by an experienced detective that the most dangerous calls I'd attend would be so-called 'domestics'. The detective had suffered a serious injury at one of these calls and I was thinking about this as I peered into the dim stairwell.

We climbed to the first floor and entered the living room of a cold, tidy apartment. The furniture and decor were a blur to me in comparison to the blank, staring face of the young red-haired woman, who was probably no more than eighteen years old, sitting calmly on a chair surrounded by ambulance staff. She had been hit on the head with a lump hammer. Her boyfriend – her assailant – had fled the scene before any of us arrived. The woman was simply gazing at the floor, quiet and very still. There was blood trickling down the back of her neck and onto the carpet. The paramedics were trying to convince her to go to hospital with them, but she soundlessly refused and nothing would persuade her.

As a young woman myself – barely twenty years old and fresh out of police training school – I stood perplexed, listening. I could not understand why any human being would refuse medical care, especially if their life was in danger.

The static crackling voices on our radios intruded on the pretence that we could stand there all night trying to convince her to do something. We could see that there was no way she was going to help us prosecute her assailant. And so we left her there, sitting alone, staring at the blood-spattered floor and went about our increasingly pressing business – me, my sergeant and the paramedics – powerless and frustrated.

'Why?' I remember asking my sergeant. 'Why won't she get in the ambulance? I don't understand.'

'Get used to it,' he replied, sighing. 'It's what *they're* like.'

By *they*, he meant victims of domestic abuse. He was not an unkind or an uncaring man: this belief – that victims of abuse behave differently to 'normal' people – arose not out of a lack of sympathy; it was just his experience of domestic violence calls. He was used to seeing victims refuse help, often time and again. He, like many others before and after him, made the assumption that as an adult woman, she had the ability and the choice to just get up and leave. He likely also assumed that getting up and leaving would free her from the abuse and from the abuser, leaving her emancipated – safe. So he thought that this person, and others like her, were not acting as any normal person would or should.

I didn't see the young woman again after that night, but I never forgot her. The question I asked my sergeant – which I felt was left unanswered – has haunted me ever since. I knew in my heart – I hoped – that as soon as we left she would tend to herself, stop the bleeding, take painkillers. Maybe cry, eventually.

I wanted an answer to the question of why she had refused help. I knew she did care about herself; she *was* normal. On this particular night, the young woman had been very 'lucky' to have survived. I don't just mean the blow with the lump hammer could have killed her – clearly it could have. I mean that her boyfriend could have made sure that she died that night.

*

I joined the police service in the early 1980s, in the wake of the Sex Discrimination Act of 1975. This was a time of great change. Until then, female police officers had been segregated from their male counterparts with separate rank structure, duties and departments. Female officers like myself began to operate side by side with men. Sexism remained deeply embedded, however, and individual forces could still make rules around what their female officers could and could not do. For example, my force did not allow me to be involved in public order policing; neither was I allowed to join the dog section (my long-held dream) or the firearms unit. But I did patrol alone and there were two female officers on every shift. It was a time when tradition and modernisation clashed and I simultaneously enjoyed the benefits of (slowly emerging) equal opportunities, and the frustrations of enduring discriminatory attitudes.

Some female officers complained about the changes: they could see problems ahead. They felt that the dismantling of the women's police departments would lead to a loss of power and influence, and they questioned whether female victims would receive a fair service under the new system. Sexist culture is not maintained wholly by men: when women were brought into mixed shifts, the male culture remained dominant, inculcating many female police officers with the prevailing institutional attitudes.

I observed at close hand the ways in which women were assessed and judged, both as victims and as professionals, and I saw the impact of those judgements. Listening to conversations among my colleagues about how domestic violence and rape allegations were and should be dealt with was a brutal education in sexual politics. It had a profound impact on me and was the beginning of a lifelong discomfort around the ways we justify violence. My decision to study homicide grew out of this discomfort. The ways we excuse or justify homicide in particular can encourage rather than deter violence.

The vast majority of murders fall into two broad categories: men who kill other men in violent confrontations; and men who plan to, and kill, their partners or former partners. These two groups dominate homicide statistics every year, in every country. 'Intimate partner homicide' – one of the biggest categories of homicide – results in the deaths of mainly women in significant numbers across the world. The United Nations Office for Drugs and Crime (UNODC) reported in 2019 that 87,000 women were intentionally killed in 2017 with over half that number killed by a partner or family member. These numbers reflect *recorded* homicides but the real number is much higher, everywhere. Femicide (the killing of women because they are women) is a serious public health and criminal justice issue. According to the UNODC men commit 90 per cent of all homicides, but they also make up some 80 per cent of its victims and this statistic is historically stable. In intimate partner homicides, however, women comprise 82 per cent of victims, with men the majority of killers. For the numbers of women who kill their partners and husbands the figures are far lower. Homicides in LGBT+ relationships are also dominated by male offenders (figures from the United States, for example, show that in 2013, 76 per cent of all LGBT+ intimate partner homicide victims were gay men killed by a male partner; in the UK around 50 per cent of male intimate partner homicide victims are killed by another man). These statistics actually tell us that the most likely danger to a man is another man, and for a woman, a man with whom she is or has been in an intimate relationship.

Since men are disproportionately the perpetrators of homicidal violence against women, and also against other men, this violence is spoken about – and often justified – in masculine terms. Women and children are seen only as supporting actors in these events and as such their characters are simplified, with victim-blaming tropes replacing all complexity. This tendency dominates in our criminal justice system, especially in categories of violence experienced predominantly by women. There are no crimes allegedly more difficult to prosecute than rape and domestic abuse. It is in these contexts that most homicides of women are justified, so domestic abuse is central to understanding the murders of women.

That first visit to the woman who sat quietly in her chair and refused to get in the ambulance is still at the core of everything I write, and every analysis I complete – because her actions and the actions of her boyfriend are fundamental to understanding domestic abuse and coercive control, and intimate partner homicides.

Thirty years on from that night and I'm a Professor of Public Protection writing a report for the coroner about the death of a woman. In this role I carry out work and research that assists law enforcement and the criminal justice system to better understand violent crime and to devise ways in which we can combat it. My specialism is in homicide, and especially intimate partner homicide. My work is quite diverse and includes helping to train police officers and other professionals in assessing threat and risk, reviewing homicides for Home Office processes, helping police with investigations and cold cases, and designing interventions to better combat homicide. This is in addition to my research and lecturing, and the work I do with families bereaved through homicide.

The case I am looking at for the coroner is about the death of a woman who killed herself after persistently reporting that she was suffering terrifying control and violence at the hands of her husband. She had repeatedly said she would not support a prosecution and therefore some people questioned whether she was telling the truth about the abuse. I had been retained as an expert witness to inform the inquest about domestic abuse and coercive control, and especially the ways that victims and perpetrators behave.

As I compile my report for the coroner, I find myself still addressing questions that I heard being asked all those years ago when I was a police officer: *Why didn't she just leave?... If it was that bad surely she'd have gone?... Didn't she care about her children?... Why wouldn't she support a prosecution?* They are all variations of: *Why won't she get in the ambulance?* The report gives me the opportunity to explain why the woman who had killed herself did not want to go to the police, and to point out some of the myths we just keep believing about victims and perpetrators of abuse. Some things have changed since my police days. And some things just have not.

*

I have spent my career trying to answer seemingly unanswerable questions: though these may be complex, they do not defy logic or explanation. My approach has always been a little unorthodox, and it would be fair to say that I have not followed a straight academic path. (For over ten years, for example, I rejected formal career progression and dedicated myself to a life operating at the edges – as the lead singer of a heavy rock band.) By the time I came to academia I had had experiences in a very hierarchical and disciplined organisation, and then a lifestyle seemingly devoid of organisation and discipline. Whatever the culture or context however, I have found that people do the things they do for much the same reasons.

The starting point I use when attempting to interpret people's behaviours is that most people will act in what they *think* are their own best interests. So instead, say, of asking: *Why won't she get in the ambulance?* I would, for instance, ask: *Why was it in her best interests not to get in the ambulance?* The factor that I believe kept that young woman from accepting help that night is the same factor that motivated her attacker to get a lump hammer and swing it at her head. It is a *pattern* that binds together hundreds of the intimate partner homicide cases I have seen over the decades.

Although acknowledged for years, it is only recently that that pattern – 'coercive control' – has been named, as described by forensic social worker Professor Evan Stark (in his book *Coercive Control: How men entrap women in personal life*). Coercive control has other names, including intimate or domestic terrorism, and is recognised by most experts in the field. Such is the predictive power of this pattern, and the terrible trauma it creates, that governments in England and Wales, Scotland and the Republic of Ireland have criminalised it, and other jurisdictions are starting to follow.

Yet coercive control is often invisible, elusive or hidden. It may be recognised in law, but that has not made it easy to recognise in practice or to understand. My recent work has been towards finding ways of making this easier – for individuals, for charities, for police services and legal organisations. Too often we try to explain coercive control, domestic abuse and homicide by assuming that both victims and abusers are acting spontaneously – without rational thought. This has grown out of the so-called 'crime of passion' explanation: a narrative of intimate partner homicide straight from the mouths of the killers and their defenders.

I have found this explanation to be a myth.

During the course of my investigations, I read what other homicide and coercive control researchers had discovered, and found it fascinating. I talked to police officers and other professionals, to victims who had escaped murderous assaults, to the families of homicide victims, and to the killers themselves. I read medical records, investigation files, diaries, text messages, social media, letters from victims and letters written by killers. I listened to telephone recordings of the voices of deceased women calling for help, and have seen CCTV footage of killers before and after their crimes. I have also reviewed homicides for government processes, advised panels, reviews and investigations, and organisations up to government level on how to develop practices to try and prevent these homicides.

By examining over 400 cases of intimate partner homicide, working in my research role at the University of Gloucestershire, I was able to build pictures of the killers and what motivates them to kill their wives, husbands, partners and even children. What I have found is that the killers are often following *patterns* of coercive control. By identifying and recognising these patterns we can track how and why risk may be escalating for potential victims – spot changes earlier to intervene and stop people coming to harm. That escalation I have organised into an eight-stage journey that I have called the Homicide Timeline.

I started sharing my findings and the conversations it inspired were remarkable. Quite quickly the timeline was being used in real time by police and others to assess risk and threat; in reviewing homicides; and in arguing for protective orders. Gradually the conversations started to change.

Research does not always get much attention, but we at the University of Gloucestershire knew that this was important. We put out a press release to try and ensure as many people would know about the pattern as possible. We hoped that the timeline would resonate with people and inspire them; however, we were not prepared for the tsunami of interest that hit us on the day the research was published. We received requests for interviews and information from across the world, and I did more TV and radio interviews than I have ever done before. The BBC online news report on the Homicide Timeline had well over a million hits in the first few weeks.

Since launching our findings, the interest and momentum has increased. I have worked with police forces, probation services, domestic abuse and stalking charities, and many more professionals and organisations with the aim of transforming the ways we think about risk and homicide. I have travelled to speak to police and professionals in other countries, and universities are incorporating the Homicide Timeline into their teaching of many academic subjects, like law, criminology, nursing, psychology and social care. Individual victims and professionals have contacted me to say things like 'I used the eight stages to successfully get a protection order', or 'I used your research to argue for an upgrade in the charging decision', or 'I used the research in a patient session to develop my understanding of the risk they faced', or the timeline helped 'me make order out of the chaos' – and I feel a glow that I never thought a piece of research could give.

This book describes those eight stages. If some of these seem familiar to you, that is the point. So often we tend to excuse or normalise forms of behaviour that in fact characterise coercive control; in many ways, we have been trained not to see the danger. The stages I have identified are:

Stage One: History: a history of control or stalking
Stage Two: Early relationship: the commitment whirlwind
Stage Three: Relationship: dominated by control
Stage Four: Trigger: an event to challenge control

Stage Five: Escalation: escalating control or the advent
  of stalking
Stage Six: A change in thinking: a change of focus
Stage Seven: Planning: planning a homicide
Stage Eight: Homicide and/or suicide

The timeline challenges the 'crime of passion' explanation that
has dominated popular understanding of these homicides for
decades – millennia, even – and that I address in the next
chapter. We are seeing a shift in the thinking around this.
The more people ask questions and have these conversations,
the more likely the crime of passion explanation that protects
killers will get weaker and weaker, until it has no power.
Understanding the stages of the timeline is a major step in
that process: it can be used to start conversations, challenge
deep-seated beliefs and help people support one another.

Over the following chapters I go through each of the eight
stages in the Homicide Timeline individually, using case histories from my work, to show what victims, perpetrators and
killers were thinking at each stage. I challenge myths through
the words and stories of the people involved. People like a
man called Vincent – because Vincent illustrates some of the
misconceptions that prevent a clearer understanding of coercive control. This was my encounter with him.

INTRODUCTION
The 'crime of passion' myth

Vincent

Murder, perhaps more than any other crime, is the crime of ordinary people.

Vincent is ordinary. He has never sought to be otherwise. His three-bedroom semi-detached house on a pleasant urban street in a nice northern town is well maintained, as is his ageing four-door estate car – precious emblems of the life he considered any man could expect. He claimed his entitlements and nothing more.

Yet, here he stood, silent and still in the darkness, dissatisfied, staring at the bland office building, waiting. He gripped the long, sharp knife tightly in his hand. For any minute now she would emerge from the door, and he was ready.

Donna's pace was brisk. Her keys had been in her hand since before she exited the building where she worked. She didn't want to hang around in the dark car park fumbling for them in her bag; she was confident but cautious. She clicked the electronic key and watched the lights of her car flash. She breathed a sigh of relief that she was at the vehicle, safe. But before she could get the door open, Vincent struck the first of many blows, plunging the knife deep into her chest. Donna died quite quickly, but Vincent kept going. On and on, inflicting thirty-eight stab wounds to her body.

*

It is over a year since that day, and Vincent and I sit opposite each other on hard wooden chairs separated only by a battered old table as we prepare to speak about the murder of his wife, Donna. Vincent is serving a life sentence for that murder. Without remorse, shame or guilt he tells me in fairly hushed tones that throughout his life he has been a victim; no one ever listened to him, and no one put him first. Just for a second his watery brown eyes fill with tears of self-pity. But I am here neither to pity him, nor to condemn him. I am here to find out if he could have been stopped.

Studying people like Vincent – people who decide to kill their wives, husbands, children, partners – is something I have been doing for many years. I study them not to treat or rehabilitate them, but to find ways of preventing others like them from killing. I would not be involved in helping Vincent reintegrate into society for example, nor would I counsel him.

Vincent was not a routinely violent man; he was not considered an abuser before he killed Donna. But he was controlling, and it was this control that revealed the danger he posed to her.

I look at him closely, hunched against the grubby magnolia paintwork that is like camouflage for him, though he is not chameleon-like; he does not change and adapt. And perhaps that is part of his problem: his utter inflexibility. It just so happens that this tired, drab room, in a crumbling grey prison, is his perfect milieu.

We are often shocked when a killer is unmasked. 'But he was such a nice guy,' friends and neighbours will say. I imagine Vincent's neighbours describing him as a quiet man who kept himself to himself, a man who was not overly friendly, but no trouble. They certainly would not have marked him as a potential murderer.

We like to think that we would know a murderer if we met one, that there would be an identifying 'mark of Cain' that our finer instincts would recognise: someone different from us, someone we are unlikely to encounter in our day-to-day lives. But when we consider that two women are killed in the UK by their partners each week, three a day in the USA, and around five a day in Mexico, then this idea starts to fall apart. These women have not only met a person capable of murder, but may have moved in with or married them. In 2020 in the UK the intimate partner homicide rate more than doubled after lockdown restrictions were enforced during the Covid-19 pandemic and similar rises were noted across the globe.

In Mexico in March 2020 there was a call for a general strike by women in outrage at the ten women a day killed in 'femicides'; in the UK the new Domestic Abuse Bill has seen campaigns for changes in homicide defences that justify intimate homicide, like 'rough sex' strangulation; in late 2019 in France, where they have one of the highest rates of intimate homicide in Europe, there were nationwide rallies held accusing the authorities of turning a blind eye (using the hashtag *Nous Toutes* or *All of Us*); in late 2019 South Africa declared femicide a national crisis, with the government reporting that a woman is murdered every three hours in the country; Pakistan is one of the most dangerous countries to live for women and such is the problem that in 2019 the Chief Justice announced 1,000 extra courts just to deal with violence against women. There is increasing international recognition of the problem of intimate homicides, a problem borne mainly by women and perpetrated mainly by men.

The killers are too often assessed by their status as husbands, boyfriends or lovers rather than as dangerous criminals. There is an assumption that either the killing is contained and wider society is not at risk, or that it is in some way justified. In my experience neither is true. There are links between domestic abuse and wider crime, there are links between domestic abuse and other forms of homicide, and there are many cases where more than one partner is killed. For example, Theodore Johnson was convicted of murdering Angela Best in 2016 but had killed two previous partners, one in 1981 and another in 1993; Robert Trigg was convicted of killing Susan Nicholson in 2011, and had killed a previous partner in 2006; Ian Stewart was jailed for killing Helen Bailey in 2016 and is also charged with murdering his first wife in 2010. Children are sometimes killed, or others who may become targets, like new partners or family members. Think of Alan Hawe, who killed his wife Clodagh and their three children Liam (thirteen), Niall (eleven) and Ryan (six) in Ireland in August 2016, or Janbaz Tarin, who killed his partner Raneem Oudeh and also her mother Khoala Saleem. Raoul Moat attempted to kill his former partner Samantha Stobbart, and succeeded in killing her new partner Chris Brown in July 2010. He also shot police officer David Rathband in the face, blinding him. PC Rathband died by suicide in February 2012.

We tend to give some killers in the public eye or in fiction a certain degree of charisma; they can become pseudo-celebrities, their names tripping off the tongue as if they were rock stars. But these figures bear little resemblance to the most common kind of murderer – the killers we are most likely to meet. These killers' names are rarely remembered, they serve sentences shorter than most of us would imagine, and they are part of our communities, working alongside us, living right by us, just like Vincent.

Vincent is a killer. He became a killer the day he murdered Donna. Before that he was just a man, but with the hidden potential to plan and execute a murder. Even now, sitting in this prison, he is essentially still the Vincent he always was. The Vincent who lived and worked among us. So the real conundrum is to try and understand what brought Vincent out of the shadows.

'I just snapped'

Vincent sits very quietly in front of me. He has a lot of hair for a man in his late fifties but it's not well kept, like his shave is clean but not close. He gives no clues that he is capable of such violence. Unlike some of the other violent men I have met, Vincent appears to lack that veneer of self-assurance: he is not commanding any space; he does not speak loudly. It would be easy to forget that he had planned the killing of his wife well in advance, and he had executed that plan efficiently and quickly. Donna was taken completely by surprise, with no chance to defend herself as she tried to get in her car. After the brutal and merciless attack, he let her fall to the floor and called 999 to confess. It is not unusual for killers like Vincent to call the police, or a friend, and immediately admit what they have done.

When Vincent was arrested he told the police: 'It was like a red mist came down, I just snapped' – giving the impression that he had grabbed a knife and stabbed Donna in a spontaneous fit of anger. But when talking to me he says: 'Nobody is listening to me; they just don't want to know how things were affecting me. . .'

'I will listen to you,' I say.

And that is exactly what I do, very carefully.

Vincent has had plenty of time to reflect on his violence, so I jump straight in to let him know exactly why I am there.

'I'm here to try and find out if anything could have been done to stop this,' I say to him, mirroring his quiet and gentle tone.

'I am the real victim,' he answers, 'but no one can see it.'

'What do you mean?'

'I had plans, you know – I was going to retire, I was going to get a smallholding and just grow my own food, maybe have some chickens. It's not like I didn't say anything.'

'So what happened?' I asked

'What always happened,' he replied. 'What I wanted never mattered – still doesn't.'

He is quiet for a while and I let the silence linger.

'No one comes to visit me, no one,' he says glumly. 'My kids, they don't want to speak to me. They don't understand. They can't see how it was. They think I'm the bad one. It's not fair.'

Vincent cannot understand why people are not on his side. Despite claiming that no one listens to him, he has been given ample opportunity to tell his story as part of the trial, and he has been talking to forensic psychiatrists as part of his defence that he 'just snapped'. What he is actually complaining about, it seems, is that no one is standing in solidarity with him. No one is saying: 'Yes Vincent, you were entirely justified in killing Donna' – and that upsets him.

'Can you understand why people might stay away, why your children might stay away?' I ask.

'It's always like this, it always has been,' he responds. 'No one takes my side, no one sees how things affect me. It just proves my point, really. I was losing everything and no one cared. She was leaving, and where would that leave me?'

I don't want to challenge Vincent's version of events. That is not my purpose. He had already spent considerable time preparing his story about what happened that night in preparation for his trial. That fiction might even have become a kind of truth for him.

I am quite happy to listen to Vincent talk about how he thinks of himself as a victim, because the more he talks, the less likely he is to draw on his rehearsed words. I also believe that he honestly feels he is a victim. I believe that he may have experienced any number of humiliations and rejections over the years. This, for him, is not just a flurry of excuses; this is who Vincent is. The interesting thing for me is not to forensically interrogate each example of rejection Vincent gives me, but to recognise the enormous role rejection and humiliation have had in modelling and shaping his internal system of status and justice. Everyone experiences humiliations and rejections; the difference is how we deal with and perceive them.

'Even my mother, she didn't like me. She never treated me right,' Vincent tells me. 'It's been like it all my life, really.'

Vincent has not yet mentioned Donna by name; he is talking much more broadly about past rejections. He then moves on to more recent injustices.

'They told me I couldn't have an allotment. I tried to tell them in court how it was, but it's like it didn't matter.'

To Vincent it is all unfair: the criminal justice system, the mental health services, his friends and family not visiting.

They all seem to him to be against him; he feels powerless to make people respect and agree with him.

But it is his inability to empathise that is the most telling. He cannot understand why his grown-up children do not want to visit. It does not seem to occur to him to wonder how they would feel about a man who murdered their mother. It is all about him. Without realising it, he has revealed a key aspect of himself, in his own words.

We learn to spot people who might present a threat to us, not necessarily by just looking at them, but by their patterns of behaviour and the way they talk about things. That is why such a substantial part of my work is listening – but more importantly, perhaps, letting people talk. There is a difference. As I let him talk, Vincent expressed in his own unpractised words what propelled him, thus allowing me to work out where the brakes might have been best applied.

*

For millennia we have rationalised the killing of spouses with the idea of a 'crime due to passion' – the *crime passionnel*. This idea neatly explains the seemingly inexplicable killing of a loved one. It encourages us to believe that people might kill their lovers or spouses in spontaneous fits of jealousy or rage, having discovered, say, some extramarital affair or terrible betrayal. This can seem plausible because most of us have experienced some rejection, or a relationship ending that was particularly painful. We can imagine how some people might, in those circumstances, lose their rationality and 'just snap' or 'lose it' by doing something completely out of character. It is certainly the way many of these murders are explained in the media and in murder trials. Similarly, we can also believe that men who routinely beat their partners in what appear to be fits of uncontrollable anger might one day take it too far; death may be the result, even if it was not intended.

So of these two dominant and seemingly simple and plausible explanations, which fitted Vincent? Had he discovered Donna *in flagrante* and responded in the heat of the moment to his overwhelming feelings of jealousy?

The facts do not support this. Vincent had ambushed Donna when she was doing something perfectly normal – coming home from work. He chose his time and place; he chose his method. He had time to think and plan; he had time to be rational; he stood in the dark car park silently waiting for her. He made the decision to do what he did. This was not a spontaneous loss of control. Neither was Vincent routinely violent to Donna. This was not 'one beating too far'.

So was Vincent the exception that proves the rule? No – as in most things, Vincent was average. He had now become your average wife killer.

Once we move past the idea that these murders are 'spontaneous', we can start to challenge the idea that they are unpredictable or beyond analysis and forensic understanding. Intimate partner homicide is, in fact, one of the more predictable forms of homicide. That predictability forms the basis for my eight-stage Homicide Timeline.

Solidarity

By saying he just snapped, Vincent suggested that stabbing his wife to death was a crime of passion. He was expecting that everyone would assent to this and believe him.

When I met Vincent, I was with a colleague. She had struggled with the notion that she would have to shake hands with him. She did not want to touch Vincent; not out of disgust, and not out of fear, but out of solidarity with Donna. She remembers his hands very well from that meeting – can still describe their large and gnarled appearance as if he were sitting before her now.

I was studying a case once where a man murdered a teenage girl who was on a school exchange trip in the UK. The girl's mother sat through the trial of her daughter's killer, a known sex offender, who was eventually convicted of that murder. At the end of the trial a lawyer from the defence team sent her a note that said: 'I promise I never touched him, I did not even shake his hand.' Like my colleague, the lawyer felt discomfort out of solidarity.

However, in my experience, in cases of intimate partner homicide, solidarity with the victim is much less in evidence than solidarity with the killer. Media reports often look for a sympathetic angle to try and explain what happened ('*he loved her so much he killed her in a fit of passion*') and this is what Vincent was expecting. However, when the victim's real story is heard, and the brutality of the violence is clear, solidarity with the killer becomes more difficult. Unfortunately, the victim's story is often lost from the official record – their experiences go unheard because they are no longer with us and cannot share their story.

'She was wrecking my life and no one cared,' Vincent tells me.

'How was your life being wrecked?' I say.

'She was leaving me, and she did not care how that left me.'

An obvious question might have been: 'How did killing her make things better for you?' But he was not trying to make his situation better when he killed Donna; he was righting a perceived wrong. This was punishment.

The fact that Vincent did not try to cover up his crime is also telling. It seems a contradiction, because Vincent called the police to confess and he appeared to take responsibility for what he had done. But admitting to doing something is not the same as accepting that what you have done is wrong. Vincent had been expecting people to think he was right, to stand in solidarity with him. He felt justified. His sense of injustice was more important than Donna's life.

Vincent does not have a mental illness – he can rationalise and function the same as anyone else. It is not even that his belief systems differ in any significant way from the society he lives in. His explanations for Donna's murder are not outlandish or bizarre; they are, in fact, what we see in press reports and legal defences all the time. They are a mix of what Vincent thinks will attract sympathy and his own sense of outrage that his needs were not prioritised by his victim.

This man was not routinely violent, so we need to look deeper, at other behaviours that are common to these killers. Talking to Vincent is only the start of the process for me; I have found that when it comes to identifying danger signs and recognising patterns, it is the people around the deceased and the assailant who will have some of the most interesting and useful information. For this reason, I spend a lot of time talking to families and friends of killers and their victims, to police officers and probation officers – anyone who knew the killer before they killed. What I have learned is that the danger signs are not always what we might expect.

Vincent was shown, by those who knew him, to be a man with noticeable 'eccentricities'. These 'eccentricities' were not considered to be dangerous, and no one described him as threatening. However, they were all about control – and focused on Donna in the main, and also their children.

Three questions

Once a relationship has been formed, the instincts we have that something is not quite right can too often be minimised. There can be seemingly plausible explanations for every potential danger sign – explanations that contrive to make us question whether they are danger signs at all.

There are three questions to ask when considering whether someone's behaviours are a problem in a relationship, as articulated by victim advocate the late Ellen Pence. First: are these behaviours part of a pattern? Second: is this pattern making someone change their daily routines or choices? Third: is someone fearful as a result of these patterns?

In answer to the first question, Vincent's family told me he was a man who had routines, and there was one they all spoke about. He had a particular liking for soap operas, and one in particular. He watched it compulsively. But he insisted that his family watch it with him. Everyone had to be at home before the theme music started, they had to watch together, and they had to stay to the end.

Second, we know that Donna had to change things she was doing on a daily basis to placate Vincent and fall in with his routines. She made sure she was always there for the start of his favourite programme, no matter what else was going on.

Third, Donna was fearful of the consequences of challenging Vincent. She complied because not complying was not worth it. They all complied to keep the peace.

There were no reports that he ever beat or hit Donna, though we cannot know for sure. Donna never said anything to suggest this; there were no unexplained injuries. However, there were lots of threats to kill himself – a concerning behaviour when used to control people.

Just because Vincent was not openly violent does not mean Donna was not frightened of him. At one point, about ten years before her death, Donna had said she wanted a divorce. She told her friends that soon afterwards some things started to go wrong with her car. A friend found that the brakes appeared to have been tampered with. She took the car and got it fixed, but she didn't tell the police. She did tell others she thought Vincent was responsible.

She told him that she had had the car fixed, and that she would get it checked over regularly now, because she was worried it could happen again. She said to Vincent she thought it was local youths; she did not accuse him. Nothing else happened to her car. Whether or not her fears were founded, this proves she thought him capable of deliberately hurting her. Donna's fears would have been generated through previous experience of Vincent, and knowing what he is potentially capable of.

I would never have got this information from Vincent – the fact that his wife and children had to slavishly follow his routines, and were monitored daily. He would never divulge it if he had tampered with her brakes.

I asked him if he remembered Donna's brakes being tampered with. He denied any memory; in fact, he looked hurt at what I was clearly implying.

This presents its own challenges for my work. Vincent is the one who, despite his claims he is not listened to, will have a defender in court – just for him, to put his side of the story – and, if necessary, to attack Donna's character. Donna has been silenced by death. Victims' families have, in my experience, few opportunities to set the record straight, or to get their loved one's story heard; families can be accused of lacking objectivity, but that accusation is rarely directed at the killer. It is Vincent who is considered the more interesting and deserving of a platform. It is a real disparity that creates difficulties in trying to prevent future homicides. The criminal justice system does not always publish victims' accounts or make their voices central to proceedings, and I believe we find out the real dangers through listening to them.

Friends and family knew that Vincent and Donna's marriage was not good and that they were not happy. Putting together a jigsaw after the event often reveals patterns and risks that seem to become clearer with hindsight. But hindsight and foresight are just different sides of the same coin: they share the same information. The difference is *when* that information is recognised or identified. So the signs that identify whether a marriage is merely bad or dangerous are, more often than not, there, waiting to be seen. Certainly, it was considered by many that Vincent and Donna were in a bad marriage, but that does not capture the reality. The reality is that Vincent was in a bad marriage; Donna was in a dangerous one.

*

It is important when hearing about cases of homicide, where those realities are over-layered with so many complexities, to never forget the real trauma of real people suffering the worst of pain. I am thinking about Donna and her loved ones as I write this. I think about how she walked to her car that night as usual, thinking she was safe, but before she could even open the car door Vincent had stabbed her, furiously. No talking, no arguing, no warning. Donna fell where she was – that is where the police and paramedics found her.

Homicide adds an extra inescapable layer of pain for those left behind, and we should not underestimate the trauma that creates. Vincent seemed incapable of appreciating the pain he had caused to his children, thinking only that they should understand *his* pain.

The trauma rebounds on professionals too. Most people working in areas of death and loss often need 'clinical supervision' to allow them to reflect on the disproportionate amount of distress and threat they may observe and experience, and to try and navigate their way through it; it is impossible over time not to be affected or changed by it.

The first time I encountered a dead body I was with the same sergeant who accompanied me to that first domestic violence call. He had sought me out as soon as this call came in: it was protocol to get new officers out to such situations as soon as possible. I was very anxious by the time we got there, though trying my best to hide it. I knew instinctively that I would leave this call a different person.

The body was upstairs, and my trepidation increased with each step that brought me closer to it. My sergeant waited downstairs. I pushed open the bedroom door where I knew the corpse to be, and stepped in. My heart was pounding. I felt spectacularly ill-equipped to handle the experience.

The deceased was a young man in his early twenties. He was suspended in a bedroom cupboard by a bed sheet that was tied around his neck. It looked as though he had been there for some hours. I felt an overwhelming urge to hold him, to comfort him. I do not know how long I stood there: it may have been five seconds; it may have been five minutes.

It was part of my job to ascertain if there were suspicious circumstances before he could be cut down and taken away. I could hear his mother downstairs, screaming – a deep primal scream that I will never forget. I could imagine my sergeant trying to calm her, and in a way I was glad I was upstairs. Later, when I went back down – as I eventually had to do – I said something very stupid that reflected my inexperience. The young man's mother was imploring me to explain why her son would kill himself: why would he do this ... had she failed so badly as a mother ... was he in so much pain? I just wanted her to be healed, so I said: 'Perhaps it wasn't suicide...' It was a simple but terrible attempt to help her.

She stopped crying for a second, and her face contorted as she took a step towards me.

'You mean he was murdered?' she screamed.

I did not mean that. I was trying, in my own clumsy inexperienced way, to suggest it could have been an accident. I thought it would help. Murder was so much worse for her than suicide, and I learned a lot about humility as a result of her response. She wrote a letter to my superintendent about me, and a week or so later I was called to his office and he read it aloud. I cannot remember the actual words she used, but I remember she apologised for the way she had shouted at me; I have never felt less deserving of an apology.

*

It was distressing for Donna's family to learn how she died, and it was important for them to have some answer to the question: why? Why was she murdered?

There is a problem-solving principle known as Occam's razor which, broadly speaking, claims that the simplest explanation is probably the right one. People will generally seek what appears to be the most plausible account for anything, and murder is no exception. However, what seems simple or plausible can change. Vincent told his story in court – but how much can we rely on court testimony to tell us what really happened? Juries like plausible explanations and Vincent would have tried to mitigate his actions and present the most sympathetic story in the most believable way.

In our adversarial justice system the best-argued story may win, and very compelling arguments can be based on discriminatory beliefs or misinformation. Sympathetic rationalisations and victim-blaming are common and can impact on the way we interpret and respond to stories of control or violence. In our court system there are only two parties to proceedings: the accused person and the state. The victim does not have specific representation. It is expected that the state will represent the victim, but the state has limits put on what they can say, and the way they can say it, because they must maintain some objectivity. We should not comfortably assume the state and the primary victim are one and the same thing. This actually leaves the victim with no particular dedicated defender in the way there is one for the defendant, and there are fewer limits placed on the defence advocate. This is one of the reasons that perpetrator stories and defences are more visible.

The danger is that what is said in court often becomes our official historical narrative, and we then try to learn from something that has little basis in fact. This is why I made the decision to talk with Vincent and some other killers – exploring why they give the explanations they do – rather than focusing on whether the explanations themselves have credence.

Vincent travelled through the eight stages that make up the Homicide Timeline. At every stage someone noticed something – not always something that they could necessarily explain as dangerous, but something that unsettled them. People like Vincent go through these stages because of the way they are, who they are, or who they have become. He did not go through those stages because of the way Donna was, or the way she behaved. This was all about Vincent.

1

Stage One: A history of control or stalking

The first stage in the timeline occurs even before two people meet and form a relationship. The interesting thing is that this stage even exists – because if it does, I am saying that people who kill their partners are a 'type'. It is not about a dynamic between two people; it is all about a controlling person. The most significant red flag that warns of danger ahead is that they are controlling, and have been controlling before.

I am rarely in my office at my desk, because much of my work requires me to be anywhere but. On one particular day, however, I was, and I took a call from an outside number.

'Is that Jane Monckton Smith?' a female voice barked at me.

'Yes,' I said, a little taken aback.

'Stop calling my husband a murderer. He's not a murderer – he was never convicted of murder, and you should not do it ... I'm just telling you.' *L276,920*

'Who is your husband?' I enquired.

'You have been talking about him, I've been told.' She then gave me his name. 'You've been talking to the family, I know you have.'

'I'm sure I have never called your husband a murderer,' I said calmly. 'He was convicted of manslaughter, wasn't he?'

'Yes he was, and that means he's not a murderer.'

After a conversation where the woman tried to convince me that her husband was a misunderstood and lovely man, we ended the call on friendly terms and I never heard from her again.

I was surprised that she did not consider the fact that her husband had killed his first wife to be a concern for her. She was right that I had been speaking with the victim's family. I had been working with a charity called AAFDA (Advocacy After Fatal Domestic Abuse) because the family were trying to raise some issues around the case with their MP and make some legal challenges. AAFDA was set up by Frank Mullane after the murder of his sister, Julia, and her son, Will. They help families negotiate their way through the formal processes that are inevitable and unavoidable after a murder, such as Domestic Homicide Reviews (DHRs), inquests and trials.

The victim in this case had been terribly misrepresented in court, and in the media, and the damage it had done to her memory, and the additional distress it caused to her family, was inestimable. There had been no trial because the court accepted a plea of guilty to the lesser charge of manslaughter. (Manslaughter does not carry a mandatory life sentence, has earlier parole and says the killer is less culpable.) The consequence of this was that the accused got to present his defence with little challenge at a sentencing hearing.

In this case, in a hearing that lasted less than an hour, the victim was described as a 'nag' who had pushed the killer beyond his limits. This story was repeated and commented on in press reports, leaving the victim for ever memorialised as 'deserving' of her fate. No evidence was presented to substantiate the slurs on her character, and the killer was shown sympathy by the judge. A well-known columnist in a well-known daily newspaper was even allowed to publish a comment saying he would have given the killer a medal rather than a prison sentence, despite him having no evidence that what the killer said was true. It is also interesting that 'nagging', whether proved or not, drew sympathy and acted as a partial defence to murder. It was even noted that the killer's distress was immediately alleviated when he killed his wife. He was able to conceal her body by burying it and maintain his life for some years before it was discovered.

Given all of this, it is perhaps unsurprising that the information my caller had about her new husband presented him as a man acting as any reasonable person might in similar circumstances. She could see the courts sympathised with him; she could see the papers blamed the victim, and from this he might appear to be less dangerous, a safe person to marry. The whole of the system was telling it that way, unchallenged. The dead woman's family had no possible avenue to balance the narrative, let alone turn it around.

If someone has a history, not necessarily of homicide, but of controlling, possessive or jealous patterns, this is a red flag. Criminal records are a good indicator, but they are not the best. Most histories and red flags are revealed by the controlling person themselves in the way they talk and behave, and by the people who know them, especially former partners.

Consider a far subtler example of someone revealing their history than my conversation with the second wife.

*

Marcie met Lenny in a bar in town. It was a place where many of her colleagues went and she considered it a safe place filled with nice people. When Lenny approached her he was charming and friendly.

'I'll pay for that drink,' he said, smiling. 'You go and sit down, I'll bring it over to you.'

Marcie thought that was nice; she thought about the lovely old-fashioned approach and got that feeling she was being looked after. Lenny was taking care of everything. So Marcie went and sat down.

Lenny came and sat next to her. He was chatty and funny and complimentary.

'Let's get you another drink,' he said when Marcie had almost finished her glass. 'Drink up – come on, slowcoach, I'm going to the bar.'

Rising from her seat, Marcie offered to pay.

'Absolutely not!' Lenny said, smiling. 'That's my job. Tell you what: you can pay next time.'

Marcie thought that was okay, she would pay next time.

When Lenny came back he started talking about relationships. He told Marcie about his crazy ex-girlfriend who made his life hell: 'Yeah, she was a real difficult person,' he confided. 'She really used to press my buttons – on purpose, so I always ended up looking like the bad guy.'

'That's terrible,' Marcie said, letting Lenny know she would never behave like that.

'Then she cheated on me. I never want to go through that again.'

And suddenly Lenny, this lovely man, was the victim of a manipulating and bad woman.

But Lenny revealed some potentially concerning behaviours and language. First, he insisted on paying; he did not suggest he would or ask if he could. He also told Marcie to go and sit down; he did not talk to her where she was or ask if she would like to sit down. He manipulated the situation so that things progressed quickly from two strangers at a bar to two people sitting together and talking over a drink he had paid for. He moved things along at his pace.

Lenny continued to manipulate things: he decided when Marcie would have another drink. He absolutely refused to let her pay, and made it seem reasonable because he told her she could pay next time – he blocked her potential objection and secured a second meeting. Marcie was in his 'debt' now, and she would have to actively refuse a second meeting, which might be awkward. He said that paying for the drink was 'his job' – testing if Marcie thinks that it is okay for men to be in control.

The conversation about his ex-girlfriend is more concerning. He says he knows his behaviour was bad, but it was his ex-girlfriend's fault. He takes no responsibility for behaving badly. He reveals that he has 'buttons' that can be pushed. There are, of course, a number of ways to interpret that small interaction. From my perspective, Lenny was controlling the interaction – the location where they spoke, the amount of alcohol, who would pay and the conversation. Lenny sent warning shots about what he expects in a relationship and made it clear he thought he was a victim of injustice, despite behaving badly. He actually revealed that he has a history.

There are so many ways that interaction could have gone, so think about why it went the way it did. Lenny did not show these red flags in a deliberate way, but show them he did. Conversations are fascinating, dynamic things. They can take a million different directions, and the language chosen will be particular to the person using it in many ways. Lenny revealed his history; he also revealed how he interpreted that history, so he was showing Marcie who he was.

Controlling people are controlling for various and complex reasons. If we accept that for some people control is important, we probably accept that control will be important in all their relationships. This is part of who they are and they will not change spontaneously. If they needed control in their last relationship, they will need control in their next relationship. If they put the blame for their behaviours on someone else, that may reveal they do not take responsibility for their actions, or that they feel entitled to act the way they do. What has happened in the past is so strongly predictive of future behaviour that we should take the time to listen to what we are being told and see what we are being shown. People can change, but blaming the 'crazy ex' for your own bad behaviour is not a sign that there has been reflection and change since that relationship.

Karl

Karl murdered his thirty-five-year-old partner Bonnie, a woman who suffered from a life-changing illness and who was mother to two children. A man with a very obvious history of control and violence, Karl was well known to the police before he killed her. In many ways he is the polar opposite of Vincent, but their patterns of behaviour are also similar in many ways.

I recognised Karl as someone operating at the edges of society – not as I had done as part of a music subculture when I was in a band, but as part of a street-level criminal subculture. So-called subcultures, whether criminal or not, create their own rules that justify a less conventional lifestyle, but their moral and other belief systems often do not differ substantially from any mainstream culture. People like Karl will justify what they do through the so-called rules of their lifestyle. I could see in his style and his manner that he was used to operating at the edges, and I was comfortable with that, more comfortable than he could possibly have guessed. To him I was just another faceless professional with no understanding of his world. But he was wrong, and that was helpful to me when speaking to him. I wanted to hear him talk and, more importantly, I wanted to hear what he chose to say to me. Karl thought he knew me, though he did not know me at all. I had to wrangle the truth from the wreckage of his lies and manipulation, and that's the real challenge.

I met with Karl for the same reason I met with Vincent, to talk about the murder of his partner – a murder that left her with injuries so bad that her body was unrecognisable.

Karl and Vincent are both controlling men, but that similarity is hidden by our myopic focus on visible violence as the only real clue that they are dangerous. Karl used physical violence to control, Vincent did not. But they both planned and executed a murder propelled by much the same reason. Karl and Vincent are representative of many others just like them.

On the night she died, Bonnie would have known she was in trouble: she had been beaten by Karl before; she could not remember the number of times. On this occasion she probably knew it was worse than she'd experienced before; she had said she believed he was going to kill her, so she probably suspected that she would not survive this attack. Karl definitely knew. He knew it with the first kick to her ribs with his heavy work boots; he did not have to hold back this time because he had already decided. He had given himself permission to kill her. The violence was far in excess of what was necessary to kill Bonnie; it was gratuitous. It is what is known as 'overkill'.

Bonnie was killed around seven o'clock in the evening and Karl knew he would have no alibi for that time. He took Bonnie's phone from her body and sent text messages from it to make it look as though she was still alive right up until about midnight. He made sure he gave himself a good alibi for after midnight. He even went to the trouble of making sure he was caught on CCTV cameras in the pubs and clubs of the town that night. He tried to make it look as if she was out in a different part of town from him. This was a clumsy attempt to get away with the murder and it was quickly proved false when Bonnie's phone was found discarded in a bin. The cell site analysis (a way of tracking the location of a phone when calls and texts are made or received) caught Karl's lies, and his fingerprints were on the phone in Bonnie's blood.

When Bonnie's body was found some days later, Karl was an immediate suspect. The police arrested him quickly, but he denied any involvement, thinking he had been clever.

It is interesting that the most commonly felt emotion after a planned murder is not fear or guilt, but relief. We expect that people would be horrified by what they have done, and if it was indeed spontaneous and passionate, this would be a reasonable expectation. But Karl's violence to Bonnie that night was not spontaneous and passionate; it was planned – calculated.

*

As a woman I have had to negotiate my physical safety without recourse to physical violence for the most part. I do not have the body strength, agility or skills to win a street fight with men much stronger and more comfortable with using violence than me. Why should I? For much of my life I have had to negotiate with potentially dangerous people so that they don't assault me. It has been quite an education, starting with school bullies, then as a police officer, and then enjoying life on the fringes in festivals and clubs. But the same could be said for many people in many jobs, and in many contexts. So we all know how to weigh up the odds.

It is very different, however, to experience a threat where the odds are hideously stacked against you, rather than in a situation when you could possibly make a good attempt to defend yourself. I think this is often something forgotten when interpreting female responses to threats, violence and fear.

One night when I was a police officer I was patrolling alone. It must have been about four in the morning. The streets were deathly quiet and deserted. I was considering wandering into the police station for a cup of tea when suddenly I saw three women running towards me. All three were shouting and agitated. 'He's got a gun,' one of them shrieked, 'back there' – waving frantically in the direction of a small side road.

I firmly told them to stay away, called for back-up and then walked towards the empty side street. As I turned into the street I could see a man ahead of me lit up by a street lamp. He was in his pyjamas and he had a gun. He began walking very slowly in my direction with the gun held at about waist height, pointing directly at me. It was a shotgun.

I stopped and stood still in the middle of the road as much from shock as anything else. I was sure he could clearly see my uniform. As far as I knew, he had no argument with me personally, or the police in general. I made no move to get closer to him and I will never know if my feet would have let me move anyway. This was the first time I had ever had a gun pointed at me. It focused my thoughts: it was as if the whole world disappeared bar the little side street containing just him and me. He kept moving slowly towards me, lowering the gun as he got closer. I could see he was distressed and agitated. 'They broke into my bloody house,' he said. 'They're a menace.'

I realised very quickly that he was talking about the three women. I also knew that this man could change his own and my life in a way that would be irreversible and catastrophic in a fraction of a second. I do not think he had the gun because he wanted to kill someone; I think he just wanted to frighten someone. I believed he was more willing not to shoot than to shoot.

In that situation, with a gun pointed at me, it would not matter whether I was a man or a woman, or even a Fifth Dan black belt. The gun is a leveller. It is a good example of the odds being hideously stacked against you.

For Bonnie it was her daily experience to have the gun that was Karl pointed at her. All she had was her skill to convince him that the trigger should not be pulled.

If you ever wonder what it is like to be a terrified victim of coercive control, just imagine the other person as a person with a gun who you absolutely believe would be happy to shoot you. Then think about how you think someone should act, or rethink what you have been told about how they reacted or behaved.

*

So, I had studied Karl and I knew his history ahead of speaking to him. He had beaten and kicked Bonnie to death in a lengthy and vicious assault. He had been arrested many times before, largely for violence, much of which was against women. Like many women when faced with a man alone, I can see Karl through a specific and sexed lens that distils him to his potential threat. This is a daily action for most women, sizing up men by what harm they might do. I actually find this helpful. It's what I want to see, and is what helps me interpret Bonnie's experience and use that information – because I will survive this meeting; I will live to tell the tale.

When I reach the prison meeting room it is empty, and I have to sit and wait for Karl to be brought from his cell. The room is quite small and would feel claustrophobic were it not for the glass windows giving a clear view to the guards standing outside. A table with four or five chairs squashed around it fills the space and leaves little room to move. A wide red strip positioned at about waist height all around the room is a panic alarm; it reminds me that should I need urgent assistance, I have only to press it.

There is movement. My attention is suddenly drawn to a large, muscular man with a shaved head wearing a tightly fitted, brilliantly white shirt that accentuates the definition of his upper body: the sharp black epaulettes on his shoulders and the keys in his hand mark him as a guard. He walks quickly along the narrow corridor, his towering frame hiding a stocky, slightly shorter man following behind. Stopping abruptly, the guard stands to one side and ushers the shorter man into the room where I am sitting. This man is Karl.

The guard stoops so he is level with Karl's eyes and points a finger in his face saying: 'Play nicely now, Karl.' He then looks at me, smiles, and steps away.

This comment is more of a shared understanding between Karl and the guard about their relative power than it is about enforcing standards of behaviour in the meeting – a game where Karl can choose to play nicely with me, or not. With this comment the power in the room has been placed with Karl. I wonder if it would have been said if I was a man. Karl's violence is not part of a game. For me the guard's comment represents a chasm between male and female perceptions and experiences of violence.

Everyone I have spoken to says that Karl is violent and threatening; his criminal record certainly supports this. He is powerfully built and physically sure of himself. I am mindful of these things as I prepare myself to talk to him and explore how he could have been stopped.

Karl fits the more conventional stereotype of a perpetrator of domestic violence. During their relationship, he had subjected Bonnie to many nasty and cruel assaults; this was a pattern for him. To think that he 'just snapped' and lashed out in a fit of uncontrollable rage does not explain Bonnie's murder. Just like Vincent, Karl planned what he did. Unlike Vincent, Karl did not confess to his crime and wait for police to arrive. When Bonnie's beaten body was found some days later, Karl lied and tried at first to deny he was responsible. Then, when the evidence cornered him, he changed his story and told the police that Bonnie had attacked him and he had been defending himself.

Bonnie was a small, disabled woman and would have presented no physical threat to Karl. The inconsistencies in his account were obvious and clumsy. The mobile phone and other evidence clearly revealed his lies, but that did not stop him continuing to tell them. The judge and the jury didn't believe him, however; he was convicted of murder and given a mandatory life sentence with a sixteen-year tariff (the number of years he must spend in prison).

Karl is now sitting opposite me. As I look into his eyes in the relative safety of the prison meeting room, I imagine how Bonnie might have felt looking at that face and having no safety net, no red security strip, no burly guard within calling distance, but still knowing absolutely what he was capable of. He looks like a man used to violence; physically he reminds me of the infamous Mitchell brothers from the BBC drama *EastEnders*. As I study his face and the way he looks at me, I understand Bonnie much better: I can imagine that I might well have made many of the same decisions that she did. Bonnie was not the problem; Karl was.

Karl is an aggressive bully and everyone knew that Bonnie was in danger. No one was really surprised to hear that he had finally killed her. I choose my words carefully when I say 'finally', because people really did think it inevitable that he would one day kill her. Not because he might decide to do it – more that he would do it by accident in the middle of a routine beating. This can protect people like Karl from being seen as determined killers. He can be represented as a victim of his own temper.

Employing violence

Violence, however, is *employed* in coercive control; it does a job for someone. It is often used to elicit a particular outcome. Karl would just let himself use violence; he was comfortable with it, and it often got him what he wanted. He chose when and where he would use it. He did not show any signs of aggression to the burly guard who accompanied him to our meeting, for example. He was showing no signs of aggression towards me. That was his choice; he was in control of himself.

It is quite bizarre how a history of violence can defend a killer from blame in this context, as Vincent's history of not using violence was used to defend him. There is no evidence that Vincent had used violence before, so when he did, it was considered that it must have been a spontaneous, uncontrollable outburst.

This reminded me of a dinner I once attended, hosted by one of the Inns of Court. The room was full of judges and barristers; I was sitting next to a very experienced lawyer, not long off retirement. He started telling me about a recent case where he had defended a man who had killed his girlfriend, and he explained his defence strategy to me. He said that the prosecution had established that the man had a *history of strangling his girlfriends*. He had done it before, so instead of seeing this as a bad thing, the barrister told me triumphantly, he used it to defend him. 'We went and found his ex-girlfriends and I told the jury: "Look, none of his other girlfriends are dead, so why did this one die? Clearly it must have been an accident. There was no intent to kill. . ."' The barrister took a slug from his glass of wine, and then, smiling, he said: 'I lost.'

The killer's violent history in this case had been manipulated and minimised in order to form his defence. Murder trials revolve on issues of intention, and many people think that there must be an intention to kill proved beyond reasonable doubt. However, in the UK the prosecution need only prove there was intention to commit grievous bodily harm (GBH) to establish the necessary intent to prove murder.

Why did this barrister think that we would find a history of such violence a plausible defence? Because we often do. When talking about the killing of partners, we like to think there is no clear intention to kill. We work hard looking for reasons to keep the myth alive.

There are many and complex reasons why we are reluctant to blame men who use fatal violence against a partner. Most of these are historical and cultural; some are psychological.

I was speaking with my mother one day and I asked her what she thought about men who kill their wives. We were preparing lunch together and just chatting about nothing in particular. 'Years ago,' she said, 'I was running a training course for professional people; it was in Wembley and people came from all over the world.'

She stopped preparing the food and looked at me.

'There was a woman from America, and she was a bit standoffish – you know, she was not joining in and she was a bit miserable. She was quite difficult, really. I managed to chat with her one evening in the bar just about whether she liked the course and that sort of thing. She told me that her husband was very angry about her coming; he did not want her travelling to England; he felt she should be at home. But she told him she did not really have any choice: she had to go on the course, it was part of her job.

'I guess that's why she was miserable,' I said.

'Yes,' my mother replied. 'But the day she got back to the States he killed her with a wine bottle.'

My mother turned away and continued chopping the food. After a long silence she concluded, with her back to me: 'He was very jealous, I expect.'

Though the story was short, it revealed many things. First, this subject has great reach – and by this I mean everyone has a story; domestic violence has touched most people in some way at some time, even if only from a distance. Second, my mother and I were talking about this violence not only across space, as this story happened halfway across the globe from us, but across time: the story happened forty years ago. It is an historically stable and persistent problem across the world. Third – and most thought-provoking for me – was how simple and easily arrived-at my mother's explanation for this murder had been: jealousy. Is murder really such a natural output of jealousy, such a plausible explanation, that it creeps into the most casual conversation? We all understand a murder explained by jealousy because it has been part of our cultural storytelling for so long. We are extraordinarily willing to excuse men's homicidal violence against their partners by accepting that they feel jealous. The so-called crime of passion writes jealousy as its main protagonist and has been guiding legal arguments and defences in murder trials for years.

In 2009, the then Equalities Minister Harriet Harman put forward a motion to remove sexual infidelity as a partial defence to murder. At that time, and in the face of fierce opposition, it was defeated in the House of Lords, with one retired judge and law lord describing the motion as 'outstandingly obnoxious', and others expressing concern that this would unfairly tip the balance against those claiming the 'crime of passion' defence. I found this not only astonishing, but rather chilling. However, legislation was passed saying that discovering an affair was not sufficient grounds to murder a partner. In 2012 judges weakened this and held that in some cases it could. These formal and high-level legal and political arguments show how deeply held such beliefs are. Why else would a move to stop people claiming sexual infidelity as an excuse for murder be described as 'obnoxious'?

There are also deeply held sexist beliefs melding here, because it is long established that men and women are held to different sexual standards, and it is men claiming this defence in the main, not least because they dominate as killers claiming the 'crime of passion'.

The evidence of Karl's violence was there in his history, but we have to look deeper and consider whether the violence was controllable or uncontrollable. There is a difference between using violence because you are comfortable with it and you find it effective, and using violence because you have no control over your impulses. If you can wait to use it, if you can plan, you are making choices.

Blame

I was thinking about all of these issues as I prepared to talk to Karl.

Sitting opposite me at the table, he did not pay me much visual attention. Indeed, throughout the meeting he never made direct eye contact for long. He had, however, come prepared, clutching a bunch of papers, which he started sorting as I began introducing myself. He glanced up briefly, looked down, and then pushed the papers towards me.

'You can help me with my appeal,' he said simply.

Clearly he had made assumptions about why I was there. I started to explain what I wanted to talk about, but he was not really interested. Karl was only interested in what he had to say.

'Look,' he said. 'I should never have been done for murder. I'm trying to tell them, but they won't listen to me. I just need to see a doctor and get a diagnosis of mental illness. It's a miscarriage of justice – that's what it is.'

There was no formal diagnosis of any mental illness that I knew of, but Karl was insistent that he was being stopped from getting the right help. He was certainly attempting to control the way the meeting was going – what I would do for him and how I would do it. I did not try to resist him; I already knew what he was like when he could not get his own way; that was not something I needed more information on.

He continued to talk about his conviction being unfair. He was presenting excuse after excuse, and reason after reason why he should not have been convicted of Bonnie's murder. He no longer denied he had killed her, but he was insistent that he should only be convicted of manslaughter, and said he was going to appeal against his conviction. He, like Vincent, was presenting himself as the real victim of the situation.

'If they had helped me,' he continued, 'if they had listened to me, then this would never have happened. It's their fault. They should have kept her away from me.'

'What do you mean?'

'I couldn't get rid of her,' he said. 'They should have told her to stay away, because she was harassing me.'

This was a spectacular reversal: it was not him who should have been stopped, but *her*. Karl's view centred on himself and his perspective completely; Bonnie barely existed as a human being in her own right. He expected everyone to interpret everything through his needs.

'They must have known, but they did nothing; they should have told her; they made it worse,' he went on. 'I couldn't believe they [the jury] went against me,' he said. 'It's like they weren't listening.'

Karl was getting agitated, but it was about the failure of everyone – the jury, the police, the doctors – to see things his way and to excuse him. There was no remorse, no consideration of any other perspective than his own.

He never mentioned Bonnie by name, other than to say, 'Yeah, it was a shame she died,' as if she had been killed in a random accident.

'Someone was going to die,' he said.

'Why?' I asked.

'Because it was always heading that way. They should have stopped it. They must have known I was being pushed that way.'

'How would they stop you?'

'They should have kept her away, stopped her winding me up.'

Karl tried to push the responsibility to regulate his behaviour onto anyone but himself. For instance, he should be protected from people who 'push his buttons' rather than people being protected from his aggression and violence. He should not be in prison; they should be stopped from winding him up. As I said, a spectacular reversal.

'You can help me put them straight,' he said.

It may seem as if Karl was attempting to control what I would do and how I thought about Bonnie and the trial, but when I looked into his cold blue eyes, framed by the thin metal rims of his glasses, I could see this was not an attempt to control me, not for Karl. I was receiving my instructions: the control was assumed.

Personality disorder and psychopathy

Casually uncaring attitudes, such as those shown by Karl, are not unusual in people who have antisocial personality disorders. A personality disorder affects the way a person thinks and relates to other people, and those with an antisocial personality disorder are often manipulative, deceitful and uncaring. This can range in severity; broadly speaking, those on the more severe end of the spectrum may be considered psychopaths. Psychopathy and antisocial personality disorders can be diagnosed as such, but are not strictly considered to be mental illnesses. People with such disorders generally have a different way of perceiving and experiencing the world that centres them. In the main, they are functioning individuals often with what appear to be normal jobs and lives. However, it is not unusual for people with an antisocial personality disorder to be controlling and abusive.

Narcissistic personality disorder is associated with coercive control and domestic abuse. The person will probably be arrogant, manipulative and self-centred; they may need or feel entitled to the admiration of others, and are seemingly devoid of empathy. They are particularly sensitive to criticism – what I refer to as being 'thin-skinned'. Even when these behaviours are obvious and causing them problems, they are unlikely to change, seeing the problems as residing in others, or being the fault of others. Narcissists share many character traits with psychopaths and these people can be abusive to live with and very difficult to leave.

Professor Robert Hare, who is a Canadian psychologist, first developed the 'psychopathy checklist' in the 1970s. It helps identify psychopaths by listing the personality traits, behaviours and histories we might expect to see in such a person. Psychopaths do not experience the world in the same way that non-psychopaths do; for them, the world revolves around their immediate needs, and they will generally do anything to make sure those needs are met. They do not feel sympathy, and find it impossible to empathise.

Professor Hare says that psychopaths live in the moment, not dwelling on the past, and not planning for the future. In their world people are largely split into winners and losers, or as Professor Hare puts it, predators and prey. Life is a war to be won.

Of course the world is not, in reality, split in this way. Even if we believe that life can be thought of as a series of battles to be won or lost, most of us would accept that 'you win some, you lose some'. Most of us do not see everything in such combative or competitive terms. We are not taking what we can, irrespective of the consequences to ourselves or others. But someone like Karl is.

People with strong psychopathic traits are rarely any good with intuitive dynamic conversations. They can certainly be manipulative and plausible, but these are often practised scripts and behaviours. They are not so good feeling their way when the script is not followed, or when they are faced with a situation with no script they know of. It is sometimes when they have to work 'off script' that they unknowingly reveal who they are, because their responses can be inappropriate and, sometimes, bizarre. This is what I find really interesting when talking to people like Karl.

There would have been a point, fairly early on, when Bonnie would have realised that Karl was not actually as nice as he first seemed: this would probably have introduced itself in moments when Bonnie wasn't playing ball with his expectations. Karl had probably learned lots of scripts to manipulate getting his own way. Some might be romantic, and others maybe violent and terrifying. Karl would have learned that these scripts bring results. To try and keep herself safe, Bonnie may have learned how to respond to these scripts. Sometimes it worked, and other times it did not.

Bonnie had been described universally as kind and caring. She had been a mother and was part of a large, close family, so Bonnie had not been short of witnesses to her troubles with Karl. They had all watched when the police turned up in the middle of the night to 'have words' with him; they had all listened to her crying as she told of how scared she was of him; they had all tried to ignore it when Bonnie had bruises to her throat and made excuses about their origin; and they had all told each other just how much they hated Karl.

Bonnie started to predict how he would respond to things, and to change her behaviour to try to keep him non-threatening. She tried to protect her family from him. He had made threats to them and even turned up at their homes when looking for Bonnie if she tried to hide, threatening if they did not reveal her whereabouts. He had even physically attacked a male relative; this meant Bonnie would not go to her family when she was scared.

By the time the relationship reaches this point it is probably too late to be able to leave it without problems. Bonnie would have been aware what Karl was capable of, and leaving him was, most likely, not an option for her. He would not have allowed it.'

I believe Karl had an antisocial personality disorder and may even have been psychopathic, though there was never any formal diagnosis. Many abusers like Karl do have such disorders, or at the very least possess those personality traits that make them callous and self-focused. I first came to this conclusion when I met the former girlfriend of a convicted murderer to talk about her experiences. This man had killed his next girlfriend and had been diagnosed as having antisocial personality disorder.

'I don't know why I'm alive,' she told me. 'I was so nearly her; I should have been her. One day you know, he put a rope around my neck. He said everyone would think I killed myself and he would never be suspected. He knew I was terrified. I really thought he was going to do it. He was smiling, he was enjoying it.'

She talked for a long time about some of the abuse he subjected her to, patterns of violence and control that repeated over and over. I was not at all surprised that she displayed some of the symptoms of post-traumatic stress disorder (PTSD). The next girlfriend's death had hit her badly. She had heard about it on the TV and the shock brought back all the trauma and fear in a sudden wave.

'I think that all the time when I was trying to tell everyone I was so scared of him and I thought he was going to kill me, it was unreal – I couldn't make them believe me,' she tells me. 'When I heard about her, the one he killed, all at once every-thing was real. I really could have been her and it was such a shock. I came so close.'

This woman was describing how at some level she was protecting herself from the reality of the world her partner had trapped her in, and when the next girlfriend died, all the filters came off, and the aftershock was terrifying for her: 'They knew he was capable of it, but they kind of looked at me like I couldn't be that scared if I kept going back. But I was too scared not to go back, if you know what I mean.'

Not all controlling people have antisocial personality disorder or are psychopaths. Many have come to be controlling for a range of complex reasons: it may have to do with things that have impacted on them in their pasts, overlaid with societal expectations and messages about relationships – especially about hierarchies within relationships. This is a complex area. Vincent's sense of injustice, for instance, going back to his childhood, may have developed in part from adverse experiences. However, I am less concerned with learning how people like Vincent and Karl came to be controlling than the fact that they are.

Both Bonnie and Donna were scared – they were both scared of much the same thing: what would happen if they did not comply with the expectations and demands of the person controlling them. Vincent appeared from the outside to be harmless, Karl less so; both, however, were capable of planning and executing a murder.

*

Gavin de Becker, who is a world expert in threat assessment, and is author of the book *The Gift of Fear*, says that 'women live with constant wariness', and that 'their lives are literally on the line in ways men just don't experience'. Irrespective of how confident or capable they are, most women do have a different relationship with fear from the relationship men have.

I recall once being used as a decoy for a predatory sexual offender. There had been a number of complaints of a lone man following women at night and sexually assaulting them. My sergeant decided that I should patrol in plain clothes in the area where the man was known to commit his crimes. I had a radio to call for backup, and my colleagues were aware of what I was doing and where I was. That was it. No one was with me and I had no weapon. I cannot imagine this happening now. I knew that help would arrive fairly quickly if I called, but at best it would probably take between five and ten minutes, and a lot can happen in that short time.

As I walked in the quiet darkness, and viewed the long footpath where the man was known to attack, I decided I did not want to do it any more. Even if they had posted a colleague at each end of the path, I do not think I would have wanted to go on.

Reality is very different from a hypothetical situation. Emotions are far less powerful when they are only imagined. A serious threat experienced is not the same as a serious threat imagined. Imagination prompts the 'I would have done this' or 'why didn't you do this?' response. It was fine for me in the briefing room to imagine that an attacker would behave differently with me than with another woman. It was easier to imagine that help would arrive more quickly than was realistically possible; it was easy to forget that I would be frightened and the extra burden that places on the body and the mind; it was easy to forget that I would be alone and the implications of that. In some ways I didn't feel able to say I was scared – how would that look?

I did stay out looking for that sex offender, but only for an hour: I really could not manage any more than that. I changed back into my uniform and continued with the patrol of that area; I felt it gave me an extra layer of protection. My sergeant should never have put me in that position alone. And not because I am a woman, but because no officer should act as a lone decoy, male or female. I think it also raises the possibility that a 'sex attack' wasn't considered life-threatening, and that the offender was considered merely sick rather than dangerous. No one was worried about my safety.

Women are taught in both implicit and explicit ways, from a very early age, that men present threats to them that they should try to pre-empt and avoid, especially in the context of sexual assaults or domestic violence.

These lessons are in the bone marrow of most women, and they normalise managing the potential dangers. One of these lessons is that the best way to stay safe is to take responsibility and avoid provoking men. It has become an urban myth that women can control violence against them through their behaviour, the way they dress, the way they speak, or how much they choose to drink. This is a dangerous myth that gets repeated in the media, in our homes and communities, and in our courtrooms. It has been given the name of 'victim blaming' in modern social commentary. It defines how societal institutions and belief systems will highlight ways in which they believe women can manage their own safety more effectively, and not 'bring it on themselves'. For example, in rape cases a woman's sexual history or manner of dressing will often be raised to demonstrate that she is partially culpable because she did not manage her own safety. This means that we expect that women must constantly plan ahead, always thinking of possible danger. It also implies that a man's history of violence or abuse will not repeat if the woman does not provoke him.

These, of course, are myths.

The controlling patterns in domestic abuse do not sit dormant until provoked by the victim. They are perpetually active.

The controlling patterns are not responses; they are systems to enforce and monitor control. Always there, always working.

Repeating patterns

The story of Rafael is very interesting. He is a good example of how controlling people repeat their behaviours and patterns, and why their history is important.

I want first to recount the story from Rafael's perspective, to show his thinking as he contemplated the breakdown of his relationship with Sofia. It is, in part, dramatised from things he himself and others involved said of the events and of his thinking. To tell it this way gives a powerful insight into the motivations and psychology of people like Rafael and the people they victimise.

Sitting alone in his featureless flat, Rafael was fuming. He knocked back the last of his coffee and stubbed out his cigarette in the overflowing ashtray. His phone said 00.14 but he wasn't even thinking of sleep. He was thinking of Sofia. It was all her fault that he was here, and not at their shared home. She knew just how to press his buttons and she knew what he would do if she did, yet she still did it. He stood slowly but with purpose: this time he was not going to let her get away with it; he wasn't going to take any more of her bullshit. He would decide when it was over, not her. He walked out of his front door and into the dark, quiet street.

At 03.04 he walked to the petrol station where he knew Sofia was working a night shift. He stood at the locked glass doors and watched her as she worked, carrying on with her life, without a thought for him and his suffering.

She spotted him through the windows and he waved and smiled. The visceral torture of the injustice he imagined he had suffered pushed him forward. Even in that moment he remembered the long black mark on the wall in their home, a scrape made by Sofia's shoe when she had crashed down the stairs during that argument. The broken cheek she suffered as a result had ensured that an ambulance was called, and the police too. That had not been enough for her, and she had made him look bad, shouting and screaming, saying he had thrown her, and that he was a bastard and a bully.

He smirked as she released the doors for him. The police had seen her for what she was though, he thought to himself; they knew she was a liar and a bitch. If they believed her, why hadn't he spent more than twenty-four hours in the cell before he was given a warning to stay out of trouble and released?

Sofia rolled her eyes and asked what he was doing there. Walking slowly forward, he smiled; he could not wait to see the look on her face when she realised.

Suddenly, he pulled her towards him and she screamed. He put his hands around her throat, stifling her screams. He knew they were out of the view of the CCTV cameras – he had planned it that way.

'I'm sorry,' Sofia managed to gasp. 'I'm so sorry.'

Some deep primal instinct told Sofia what to say. All her past experiences of Rafael hurtled through her brain's filtering systems in less than a fraction of a second.

For some reason, on that particular night, at that particular time, it was what he wanted to hear. He stood over her and listened as she tried to make things right. For some reason, on that particular night, at that particular time, Rafael stopped, convinced he had managed the situation and he was back in control.

Rafael asked for a packet of cigarettes.

At 03.36 the police arrived; a passerby had heard the screaming and called for help.

Rafael was arrested, and a furious and terrified Sofia screamed at him as he was led away to a waiting police vehicle.

There is still a strong belief that domestic abuse is a couple's problem and not the dangerous behaviour of an individual. I have heard professionals saying they must not take sides in such disputes, as if they are only about arguments and not campaigns of control. A history should not be ignored in favour of seeing control and abuse as arguments between two people, with each having equal responsibility. This would be a miscalculation.

Sofia took out a restraining order.

When he met Orla one month later, Rafael told her all about his crazy ex-wife who had called the police and told lies about him. Orla was sympathetic; she had heard lots of stories of bad break-ups. Orla did not know the significance of what she was hearing, but there was a little niggle of discomfort, and that was her intuition telling her that she had seen something in Rafael she did not trust, but she felt judgemental and churlish listening to her intuition, so she put it to one side.

Orla found that after a while Rafael was a difficult man to live with. He did not like her family, and they did not like him. He wanted to control everything she did, and she found herself living a life walking on eggshells. One day Orla decided enough was enough.

'It's over,' she said. 'Neither of us are happy, and it's just making both of us miserable. It's time to move out, Rafael. We both know it really, don't we?'

Rafael disagreed and tried to get Orla to reconsider, but she was firm and kind. Rafael moved out, but he was seething. He told his friends that he knew there must be another man and he was going to find out what was going on. He said he wasn't going to accept it.

One night Rafael made sure he 'bumped into' Orla when she was out drinking with her friends. He walked over to her and said hello. He asked if he could 'have a quick word'. Orla was a bit irritated, but rather than endure the embarrassment of arguing with him, or humiliating him in front of everyone, she agreed to go outside, sit in his car and talk, for one last time. Her body was found two days later.

He had regained control – he had reset the balance; he had won. Rafael was arrested quite quickly at the carpet shop where he worked, going about his life as if nothing had happened. His colleagues stood open-mouthed as he was led away. He didn't deny killing Orla, but he told police she needed to learn she couldn't treat him like that.

The power of history

Someone's past is important because, contrary to what we often think, problems like the ones created by, say, Rafael are part of *him* – not part of a unique dynamic between him and Orla, or him and Sofia. It was not Sofia who made the problems, and it was not Orla. It was Rafael, and he would make those problems wherever he went, whoever he was with. But Rafael saw the problems as residing in his partners; he felt he was the victim, and he had suffered an injustice. Rafael had actually travelled through the eight stages twice that we know of: that is quite a history.

Such is the predictive strength of someone's past abusive, controlling or stalking behaviour, that the police can decide to disclose to new partners the dangerous behaviours from a person's past. Also, partners now have the right to request such information from the police if they are concerned or suspicious. In the UK this scheme is popularly known as a Clare's Law disclosure, after the campaigning by the family of Clare Wood, who in 2009 was fatally strangled and set on fire by her former boyfriend, George Appleton, who had a history of violence against women. Clare's father has said he believes she would still be alive had she known the full extent of George Appleton's past abuse.

Karl's history was revealed to Bonnie; the police felt that she should know he had been imprisoned for serious assaults on previous girlfriends. But knowing someone is dangerous is one thing; leaving safely is quite another.

Unfortunately, our justice system gives no guarantees: just because someone is arrested, or charged, or even convicted of a crime, does not mean that a victim is protected. When victims make a big challenge to a controlling perpetrator, they are taking a risk. They need to know they are prepared and protected; they need to trust the system more than they fear the consequences of leaving, and that can be a big gamble. No one can guarantee what will happen in the courts, and if we add in the secrecy and inflexibility of the family courts, it is little wonder that victims withdraw complaints and go back to trying to 'manage' their own safety.

However, it has been found that there are much better outcomes, where victims do engage with the police and the justice system, when the system does what it is supposed to do. It is all about the skills of the professionals, the trust of the victim, and the system using the powers it has. Services have improved significantly compared to when I was a police officer. I have been involved in helping develop specialist units to assess and manage risk and danger. There are new orders like Stalking Protection Orders in the UK, and legislation that has criminalised abusive patterns in many places. There is growing recognition of non-violent abuse and control, and growing awareness of the risks of stalking. There are dedicated victim advocates and case-risk conferences. Professionals are far more aware of the difficulties faced by victims, and there are many skilled and passionate people who are dedicated to supporting victims of coercive control and stalking. There is still much work to be done. We could improve the ways in which the powers we have are used to manage controlling people, and raise the recognition of controlling patterns in this context. The most significant changes will come when we recognise that controlling and abusive people are dangerous, and not merely in a bad relationship.

It is often argued that people should be given a chance to forget their past and their history and start afresh. It is also sometimes argued that someone's history is their own business. In the context of coercive control and stalking this argument may be more compelling if those people have had some intervention that addresses their issues. No intervention means no change, and that means the patterns will repeat. These are patterns, not silos; that is, they are not contained incidents or events that have no relationship to future or past events.

A domestic abuse register

In January 2018 a campaign was started by Len Duvall of the London Assembly to set up a domestic abuse register, similar to the sex offenders register. It was taken up nationally by campaigners like Samantha Shrewsbury, the mother of seventeen-year-old Jayden Parkinson, who was murdered by her former boyfriend in 2013. I believe a register is a good idea and I have supported this campaign. Used properly, a register could be helpful in identifying some of those people who are potentially dangerous, while sending a message to them and others that there is no solidarity from society.

However, many controlling people never come to the attention of the police or the courts, so would never end up on a register. Vincent's patterns of control only came to the attention of the police after Donna died. Many victims never call the police. So from this perspective we would have to accept that a register would not contain *all* repeat abusers – it would not capture *all* high-risk persons – but it would be a good start in identifying so many of those who are controlling and letting them and others like them know they are on the police and society's radar.

A register would tell us that everyone on it is at stage one of the Homicide Timeline. It might also start to change the conversations and make clear that these people repeat their patterns, and are dangerous. Right now we make no such declaration, and that needs to change.

Making a history visible: reporting
abuse and control

I was at the Crown Court in a city in the south of England one day, observing a trial. The court was quite empty: just the legal teams, and two or three members of the public, who I suspected were related to the primary victim in the case. A man called Martin had been charged with assaulting his girlfriend and it was going to be very difficult to convict him, despite his history.

Dressed in a plain, pastel-blue shirt, his hair neatly brushed, Martin sat in the dock, surrounded by glass. He was directly facing the judge, with the jury to his side. He sat still most of the time, but would occasionally write notes onto a pad, and tap the glass to get the attention of his lawyer. He had pleaded not guilty.

The prosecution argued that on the night in question Martin and his girlfriend were in a pub they regularly frequented. They had been arguing, which, according to witnesses, was not unusual. The argument continued in the car park as they left, and at some point it was alleged that Martin got into his car and drove it at his girlfriend. It was further alleged that he got out of the car and put his hands around her throat and started to squeeze, but ran off as others approached. His girlfriend had some injuries to her lower legs and some red marks on her neck and throat. These were recorded in photographs.

The prosecution argued that Martin was a man who used violence regularly and presented a real risk of further serious violence to his girlfriend. Martin denied this. His defence team argued that his girlfriend was vindictive and her complaints of domestic abuse were made up because she wanted revenge on Martin for leaving her.

Martin's girlfriend was called as a witness. I watched her walk across the courtroom, not like a triumphant winner halfway to the end of her game of revenge – not at all like that. When she stood in the witness box, there was no expression on her face. She stood fairly straight and her hand was out in front of her, resting on the wooden edge. She did not look at Martin.

The prosecution lawyer started to ask her questions about the night Martin had assaulted her.

'I can't remember,' she said with no expression on her face.

'But you called the police, didn't you?'

'I really don't know what happened that night,' she responded. 'I just can't remember anything.'

Martin was staring at her, arms folded.

'But you gave the police a statement that night,' the prosecution lawyer continued. 'Shall I read it to you?'

'I don't care what you do, I just don't remember,' she said defiantly.

She did not look at Martin the whole time. All through the questions from the prosecution, and all through the questions from the defence.

The lawyer had asked the judge that she be treated as a 'hostile witness'. This is when a witness does not want to give any evidence, and may even seem to be lying to the court. It means they can be treated differently.

I could feel that no one in the court had warmed to Martin's girlfriend. They may have thought she was lying about what happened, they may have thought she was scared of Martin, but no one believed she could not remember a thing. Martin's girlfriend was probably alienating herself from the jury.

Then another witness was called, a friend of them both. She was giving evidence about what happened that night and what the couple's relationship was like. She was quite confident and seemed to be trying very hard to be neutral, as though she did not want to take sides. She told the court that Martin was routinely violent and aggressive. She said the couple would have fights all the time, and she said she just wanted to tell the truth.

As she left the witness box she had to walk past Martin. They looked at each other and she smiled at him; I watched as she mouthed, 'Sorry, love,' to him as she walked past. She seemed conflicted. I guessed that she liked both of them.

Why did this woman feel conflicted? Why didn't Martin's violence cause her to dislike him?

When I was a police officer there was a man who was known to be highly dangerous. Physically very big and strong, he was always starting arguments with people, and would assault people just because he felt like it. He would walk into a shop or a pub and just start trouble with someone. He was controlling and abusive to his girlfriend and his children. Whenever a call came in that this man – who I will call Stevie – was involved in a confrontation, we never sent less than four or five officers to deal with the arrest. But despite this, some officers felt it a badge of honour to claim that they understood or liked him. There was a grudging respect between some of the men that I simply did not share. I remember one officer bragging openly that he had a special relationship with Stevie, that they got on well. This may have been a misplaced attempt to share in the 'reflected glory' of Stevie's reputation. His violence was not, for some of my colleagues, a reason to condemn him. I still do not fully understand why we are so forgiving of such brutality. In most cases it will be because people are not one-dimensional; even brutal, nasty people may have a more reasonable or 'nice side'. What concerns me is that failing to hold these people to account, or sympathising with their repeated violence, can look like solidarity.

I remember seeing Stevie up ahead of me one day. It was about two o'clock in the afternoon and my shift had just started. He had a very distinctive appearance, mainly because he was so tall and walked in a very aggressive manner. I had a feeling in the pit of my stomach that made me want to turn around and walk the other way. Of course I would not have done such a thing. I continued walking towards him, wondering if he could resist starting trouble with me. He was still quite far ahead and had not seen me, when all of a sudden he ran into the middle of the road and 'drop-kicked' a car driving towards him. The car swerved out of his way and luckily there were no injuries. I sighed and a feeling of gloom enveloped me. I immediately called for back-up before even speaking to Stevie, because I knew I was going to need to arrest him, and I knew he would see that as a challenge to overcome, even though I am only five foot four and he is well over six foot and burly. An elderly woman approached me and pointed at him, shouting: 'What are you going to do about that, then?'

I approached Stevie, who was just standing there laughing. As soon as I opened my mouth his hand shot out, he grabbed my collar and, close up, just stared at me. It was a difficult moment. The woman was still standing watching. I knew I could not force handcuffs onto him on my own – however, neither would any of my male colleagues in the same situation; this was going to take numbers. So, I looked at him and spoke very quietly.

'Stevie, this isn't making either of us look good.'

He let go, but continued laughing.

'Are you going to let him treat you like that?' the elderly woman shouted over.

'It's all fine, don't be concerned,' I called back, keeping my eyes firmly on Stevie.

At that point my backup arrived in the form of a Transit van, travelling at high speed with blue lights flashing. Far from being intimidated, Stevie ran at the van, inviting a fight. About ten police officers tumbled out of the back and managed, after much fighting, to get him handcuffed and into the van.

I spent much of the rest of my shift wondering what he put his girlfriend through, and when I had cause to interview her not long after, on an unrelated matter, I was able to find out. She had made an allegation that Stevie had hit her. She also wanted to get a restraining order to keep him away. She described him as 'a complete nutter' and, with some anger in her voice, said: 'He's not scared of the police. I don't know how to get away from him.' Her mother was with her and was just as frightened of Stevie, but the two women were determined to go to court.

I accompanied them, and I remember the anxiety I felt going to the magistrates' court to give evidence against Stevie; it would have been nothing compared to the anxiety they felt. Imagine defying a man who can only be taken down by a van-load of police officers. This was a very similar situation to what Bonnie experienced with Karl. It is easy to imagine why victims would, in such circumstances, withdraw their allegations. The consequences of challenging a controlling person are not always violent, but are often threatening or traumatic.

I checked up on Stevie recently. I found that he has a number of domestic violence convictions and is a suspect in the murder of a woman found beaten to death, though he was never charged; he has hundreds of offences on his record. Not too dissimilar to Karl.

*

At the Crown Court, where Martin had pleaded not guilty to assaulting his girlfriend, it was revealed to everyone in the court that he was subject of a life licence for the murder of his first wife by strangulation.

When someone is sentenced to life they only serve part of that sentence in prison. The number of years they must serve in prison is called the tariff. The rest of the sentence will generally be served out of prison on licence. This means that they can potentially be called back to prison at any time, should they break the terms of their licence. The only exception to this is when someone is given what's known as a 'full life' sentence. This type of sentence is rare and there are only about fifty of these prisoners in the whole of the UK, including the late Peter Sutcliffe (the so-called 'Yorkshire Ripper') and Rose West. These prisoners will never be allowed out on licence.

Martin had been released from prison two years earlier, having served his eight-year tariff, and during this time he had met his new girlfriend. He told her about his conviction, and all about the injustice of it.

Should the knowledge that Martin had murdered his previous partner make any difference to the way we feel about Martin or his girlfriend? It certainly impacted on me and the way I thought about the case. The trial was stopped for legal reasons after the pathologist gave evidence. The court was told that it was necessary to start the trial again without anyone being told about Martin's previous conviction, because the murder of Martin's first wife was not regarded as similar enough in circumstances to the second allegation for it to be revealed to the court. It was argued that no one should know about his history because it would be unfair.

This forces us to look at Martin's behaviour as an isolated incident, and does not acknowledge the significance of his patterns of behaviour and his history. The judge was unhappy with the way things had gone and made this known to the court when he commented that Martin would probably escape justice. I do not know if there ever was a retrial for that assault.

So creating a formal history is not as simple as we might think; convictions for coercive control are low, as are all domestic abuse-related offences. All the more reason to listen to what those with experience of such people and their controlling behaviours tell us. It is in all our interests to do this. We should think about someone's history of abuse and control in terms of what that means for their future behaviour. It is important, not only because it may help us assess risk, but it also helps us predict who may be dangerous.

I often find histories of controlling patterns when I research cases. In a recent suicide of a young woman, for example, I was writing a report for the family, and there seemed to be general agreement between friends and the police that the husband was not a factor in her taking her life, that he was a nice, run-of-the-mill type. I was not convinced and neither were her family, so I started to dig into his history to get a sense if he was the 'type' of man to be on my timeline. I found some very interesting information from those who had known him for a long time. He did indeed have a history of controlling and obsessive behaviours that some people had found deeply disturbing. We also found evidence that he had threatened to kill his wife in the past, and had made a serious and reckless attempt to do so. But none of this history was documented in any official way. Controlling people are sometimes very good at stopping their victims speaking, and manipulating the way they are perceived by professionals.

So stage one is all about history. Does the person have any history of stalking, control or violence? Are they the type of person who has to win? Are they routinely jealous and possessive? These are all red flags. Take any hint of a history seriously; never assume it's all a misunderstanding or maliciously concocted by a vengeful ex. Just be open to the potential for the person to be at stage one of this timeline.

2

Stage Two: The commitment whirlwind

I went out for a drink one night recently. It was late December, and as I took a sip from my festively spiced drink and surveyed the crowded room, I thought how much I liked Christmas. The cold weather, the dark evenings, the coloured lights and deep evergreen foliage always encourage a full flood of childish nostalgia in me. I was happy watching hitherto formal and collegial relationships descending into informal shouting and dancing across all of the gathered office parties in the room, when very unexpectedly a man dressed as Santa burst through the doors and loudly blew a whistle, bringing the room to silence. Everyone turned their attention to him. He very purposefully and slowly walked towards a young woman standing with a small group of her colleagues. She barely moved, her face not quite finding the right expression as she tried to work out what was happening. Suddenly Santa dropped onto one knee, leaving little doubt as to what would follow. With a grand flourish he pushed a small velvet box towards her and boldly claimed to everyone that she was the love of his life and they would be together for ever if she would just agree to be his wife. The silence hung heavily as we all waited for her response, and joy erupted like an explosion as she enthusiastically agreed.

My warming nostalgia abandoned me.

Now, irrespective of the romance and the timing, or whether it was a lovely gesture, we have to consider the pressure on that woman to say yes. I was probably the only person in the room, at that moment, feeling a sense of dread instead of joy. What concerned me was she had nowhere to turn; she could say yes and give a very public commitment, or she could humiliate him and say no.

She left not long after with Santa dragging her towards the door as she pulled on her coat, still laughing, abruptly ending her Christmas night out with her friends and colleagues.

I asked about the woman when the opportunity presented itself in the ladies' toilet later that evening: 'Wow, that was pretty spectacular,' I said to a group of her friends.

'Isn't it wonderful!' a young woman enthused. 'They only met a few weeks ago – so romantic.'

Now it could be that this was *not* stage two of a coercive control journey; I am perfectly willing to accept that and hope that it was the meeting of two perfectly compatible people declaring their mutual love. But my finely tuned instincts just niggled, and my skin tingled with doubts.

We have all met people who say 'it's moving too fast', 'you hardly know each other', or 'slow things down'. Most people at some time have felt a little concerned about a relationship that seems to be travelling at the speed of light. Often their concerns are met with 'but they're so in love', or 'it just feels right', or 'it's like we've always known each other'. This rarely quells the concerns, however. We instinctively feel that it is best that people get to really know each other before they entangle themselves in one another's lives.

Stage two is when a controlling person finds someone they want to be in a relationship with and they try to move things very, very quickly, or they may be very persistent.

I remember meeting Tori's parents when I was advising a homicide review panel into her murder. They were able to tell me things about the way Tori had met Finn, the man who killed her, that you would not see in press reports or in official police records. They knew Finn, they had spent time with him, and they knew their daughter and had watched how the relationship developed and how Tori had responded.

It was a mutual friend who had introduced the pair, and that introduction happened on social media. The friend told Tori that a good-looking young man she knew had contacted her to say he really liked Tori's Facebook pictures. That young man was Finn, a soldier stationed abroad who was due back in the UK within weeks. They started chatting online and they seemed to get on really well. That was the beginning of October; by the end of the month, Tori and Finn were telling their friends and family that they were in an 'exclusive relationship' together. At this time they had not even met.

By the first time they actually met, they probably felt they knew each other well. But Tori had never been in Finn's physical presence, and she had never had a chance for her instincts to size him up, to interpret his body language, facial expressions, tone of voice or other physical features. These things are a fundamental part of our inbuilt safety systems. We can take messages at an unconscious or conscious level from our instincts that may alert us to things we are uncomfortable with or that concern us. By the time Tori had her first meeting with Finn those instincts may have been dampened.

The main reason people tend to move quickly into a relationship is because they feel themselves to be in love. The more passionate or intense the feelings, the more quickly things may happen.

Love

Research into the way we feel when 'in love' suggests that there are few cultural differences across the world, or across time, to the way it is described and felt. It is sometimes experienced as a 'grand passion' with intense feelings of attraction, and the production of high levels of dopamine and oxytocin that can give a feeling of elation. Consequent dramas or extremes of emotion are explained away as normal or expected, and the speed with which passion can take over is thought to be almost instant.

We actively seek to be in love and sometimes wait for the grand passion to hit as confirmation we have found 'the one', the person we should spend the rest of our lives with, our one and only soulmate. It is a time when both parties may be idealising each other, and forming associations and dependencies that may be very difficult to break. In Western cultures it is seen as a human right to marry the person you are in love with – so the message from the most powerful levels of society is that love is not only morally right, and a state we seek to be in, but is also the only real and legal basis for a marriage. We are told it is not acceptable to marry for other reasons, such as gaining citizenship rights, or for financial gain, for example. It gives us full permission and even encouragement to act on passionate feelings, even if that is recklessly.

In some cultures, however, arranged marriages are more the norm, with love being seen as something that will naturally develop across time. So love is important, and whether it is present as a grand passion, or between two people who come together hoping it will grow, we see it as something that should underpin a long-term committed relationship like marriage.

The problem really begins with the way marriage is the ultimate template for a relationship built around love. There is an almost universal agreement that marriages are for life. This is a powerful script underwritten in law, religion and culture, and has great relevance at stage two of our timeline.

When you commit to marriage, the expectation is that you will be committed for life. Some people can take that literally, and it may form their view of the rights marriage or a relationship bestows. The problem is that the chemicals producing feelings of 'real love', which can give controlling people so much influence, rarely last as long as the relationship.

So two things are driving stage two of this journey, and they are speed and commitment. Relationships can begin very quickly with the aim being to secure a commitment. Controlling people expect that commitment is *to them* rather than *from them*, and for life.

Astrid

I met with Astrid to speak about the death of her partner Loki. Astrid met Loki in a pub one night; they had known each other some years before, when they worked together in a bar. Astrid had been bar staff and Loki was a doorman. They had a good time, and Astrid told me they drank too much and he ended up going back to her home for more drinks. 'One thing led to another,' she said, and he stayed the night. He stayed the next night too, and then the next. Within a week Loki was all but living with Astrid.

'It just happened,' she told me. 'It wasn't like we made a decision. It just happened. That's not to say there weren't problems because of it.'

So Astrid and Loki were living together and in a relationship almost from that first night.

Astrid knew Loki had a history – she had seen him get into fights at the pub where they used to work – but thought this was because he was a doorman. Even so, she said she believed him when he also told her his ex-wife had made up lies about him having a bad temper. Astrid thought it would be unfair to judge him without giving him a chance. She told me that in some ways she thought he was being very honest and open with her; she felt he was confiding in her, and that this was trust. In some ways she felt a responsibility with that trust.

Looking back, she now thinks she should have tried to slow things down. But by the time she realised he was violent and controlling it felt too late to do anything about it. In fact, she thinks that point may even have been reached in that first week.

'I couldn't just kick him out. It was a mix of, like, being scared of him, and feeling guilty too. I would be making him homeless. I really thought that if I loved him enough and made him feel secure, then he would change. But no amount of love would have been enough, because love wasn't the problem. He was the problem and I couldn't see it at first. He was too unpredictable. I wanted him to be the nice Loki all the time. But looking back, the horrible Loki was the one who decided everything, the one who changed everything, and the one I kept waking up next to. As time went on I thought the only way out was if he killed me. I was wrong about that, wasn't I?' she said.

Loki was killed in a fight with another man who had stepped in to protect Astrid when Loki assaulted her. Sometimes things can take unexpected turns and other people can get hurt. Friends, relatives and children can get hurt or killed if they challenge the controlling person, or if they can be used in a campaign. This is especially true of children.

Loki managed to get the relationship to move at a speed he was comfortable with, and that was quite a speed. He got himself into Astrid's bed and her home and, like a cuckoo, pushed everyone else out.

I learned to drive in an automatic car and I remember my instructor telling me about something she called the 'creep' that is present in all automatic cars. This means that the car will move forward very slowly even if you do not apply pressure to the accelerator, but you do have to apply the brake to stop the car. It is a good analogy for the way coercive control starts. At the beginning, controlling people have a 'creep speed' that will keep them (and you) moving forward unless you apply the brake. If you do nothing, they creep forward on their journey imperceptibly, taking you with them. At some point, when the accelerator is applied, the journey may get very fast very quickly. The faster any journey then gets, the greater the implications of suddenly hitting the brake, as in a car journey, and that is the point. They do not want you to hit the brake. Coercive control is designed so that, for the victim, hitting the brake is a high-risk strategy.

When there is no grand passion

Not everyone who gets into a relationship will feel a grand passion. I met Tricia Bernal when I was working with her charity Protection Against Stalking (PAS). Her daughter Clare was murdered in 2005 as she was working one evening at Harvey Nichols in Knightsbridge. Michael Pech, a former boyfriend of Clare's, walked into the store and shot her multiple times at point-blank range in the head and face, killing her instantly. He then shot and killed himself.

Tricia tells me that Clare was flattered by the attention from Michael Pech, but the attention very quickly became claustrophobic and the control intense. They did not move in together or have an intense relationship that Clare thought would be for life. The intensity was in Pech. They had met when both were working at Harvey Nichols – he working in the security department, she in the cosmetics department. After about three weeks' dating, Clare decided she wanted to end things, as she found Pech too jealous and controlling. He had already decided in his own mind that Clare had made a commitment to him, even though that was not her understanding of the situation. His stalking started almost immediately and was an extension of that over-investment and control. It was so intense he was dismissed from his job. He left the country, purchased a gun for the purpose of killing Clare and smuggled it back into the UK.

Speed and commitment

Relationships with controlling people may start very quickly, but as concerning as the pace might be, it is not necessarily the most worrying thing. It is true that they like to speed things up, but their real goal is to get a commitment. For them a commitment is like getting their partner to sign an airtight contract that gives them rights and their partner responsibilities.

Most people are completely unaware of the significance and consequences of giving commitment to someone with control issues; it is risky because in the controlling person's head the commitment can never be withdrawn. Only they can end the contract, and in a way that suits them. They can see relationships as practices in possession. Society and culture actually reinforces this, as splitting up is not only difficult, it is *made* difficult. Divorce requires a legal process; it attracts blame; it is seen as failure; it is argued that it hurts children.

Historically, cultural, legal, religious and societal messages have made explicit to men in particular that control of their wife is a right, and in some places it is still a legal right. History also tells us that there were times when once a woman committed to marriage, divorce was very difficult, or even impossible. For example, there used to be a legal concept in the UK known as 'feme covert' (a covered or hidden woman) that subsumed all legal rights the woman may have had before marriage into her husband's legal persona. This tying of women to individual men for life is a cultural ideal, still practised literally in some places, or figuratively in others. It certainly has some resonance in relationships dominated by coercive control. Professor Neil Websdale, who has studied the behaviours, beliefs and motivations of men who commit familicide (the murder of their wives and children) says that these cultural beliefs are deep in the bone marrow of not only controlling men, but our cultures and societies. 'No fault' divorces are still relatively new in some places; in others they do not exist. We should not underestimate the reach and influence of these belief systems in our modern cultures. Men who kill their partners are very likely to say: 'If I can't have her, no one will.'

If a commitment to a relationship and the terms as perceived by a controlling person were in a written contract, they would probably never get a signature. The terms of these contracts are often implied in the beginning, and the metaphorical signatures are coerced and manipulated in a focused PR campaign designed to disguise and conceal. For these controlling people, in many cases, the commitment is *to* them, rather than *from* them, and they often do not feel any obligation to reciprocate as time moves on.

Sally Challen killed her husband in August 2010 after thirty years of paralysing and cruel coercive control. When the full circumstances of that coercive control were revealed in her appeal, eight years after her conviction for murder, we got an insight into these virtual contracts. Sally's husband had actually put some of his terms into writing in an email to her (for example, Sally was to agree never to interrupt him when he was speaking). This goes beyond mere possessiveness and reveals how some prioritise their own needs and desires above all else, and how strong their sense of entitlement can be. Sally's son, David, who also lived with that control from his father, stood by his mother and fought to have her murder conviction reduced to manslaughter. He was successful in 2019, with help from the Centre for Women's Justice, who represented Sally.

I have called stage two the *commitment whirlwind* because commitment is the real game changer. A critical question, then, is what constitutes a commitment? Again there are differences between individuals. Some may see having sexual relations as indication of that commitment; some may see it as an engagement ring or marriage certificate; some may take it from an implied intention to have a long relationship. Whatever the defining moment is, jealousy or possessiveness are often an indicator of concern. Use of possessive language can be a clue, for example, saying things like 'you're mine' or 'you belong to me'. A partner may talk in absolute terms – things like 'we will be together for ever'. This type of talk can be interpreted as being about love, but it is more often a sign of a possessive nature.

Many people feel flattered by jealousy; it may make them feel loved or special, and this can be powerful. This would also be a mistake. Excessive jealousy and possessive patterns are never good signs; it is always a warning that the jealous person may be unable to deal with rejection, or may perceive their partners as belonging to them, literally.

Once controlling people feel they have a commitment, and the rights they feel that bestows, they will seek to get compliance from their partner to things they see as proving and establishing that commitment. This will be an ongoing process throughout the relationship, and that is the heart of the process of coercive control in an intimate relationship.

Who is a victim?

A question I get asked frequently about this stage of the journey is around who is likely to be a target. Victims are represented across every demographic: age, class, socio-economic status, educational achievement, gender, race, ethnicity, sexual preference, religion, physical ability or employment; no one is completely immune. All personality types are represented too, so it is much more complicated. However, because controlling people, in the main, will want a rapid commitment, they may target people who they feel might give that. This does not necessarily mean a specific personality type – it could be as simple as someone they can get access to, with an opportunity to manipulate them. There are some people who may seem more suitable as partners, and this too can be for many reasons – they may live alone and have ready-made accommodation and no barriers, for example. Sometimes just smiling at someone can indicate you will not outright reject them and will be polite, so that gives them a chance to manipulate. They may have an opening for a conversation, like dog-walking, for example; they may know something about you and use that to open a conversation. They may already know you and have a perfect opportunity. They may know about vulnerabilities and make it seem as if they care.

Once a conversation is started, it is easier to find out information, not only about you as a person, but maybe also a phone number, a workplace, the school the children go to, and so on. If they find the person lives alone, access is much easier. If they are introduced to friends, children or family, if they know the person's car, this will reveal more about the person they ultimately wish to control. So from this perspective anyone could be a target.

It is a fact that women in particular are often socialised to be friendly and polite. Not all women are, but women usually try to reject men whose approach is unwanted in the most friendly and least humiliating way they can. This may be in part through socialisation, but also experience – after all, women have to be very careful how they respond to approaches from men. Being rude or abrupt can result in verbal or physical abuse.

A young Frenchwoman, Marie Laguerre, was sexually harassed on the street by a man in July 2018. Ms Laguerre says she told the man to 'shut up' or similar, but he took offence at that. The encounter was caught on video: it shows him picking up an ashtray and throwing it at her, and then following her and slapping her. Marie Laguerre posted the film given to her by a local shop owner on Facebook, and there was an instant and massive response worldwide. The French government brought in legislation allowing instant fines for harassment on the streets as a result. But more than the response of the government or the public, the point I make is about the response of that man who attacked that young woman for daring to talk back to him. It's not isolated.

I once attended an event that was organised to raise funds for a local domestic abuse service in Essex. It was held in a beautifully decorated marquee and there were lots of people there who were working with victims of coercive control. I was giving a talk designed to raise awareness of some of the problems faced by victims. I gave my talk and afterwards I was chatting to a couple of the women who had organised the event. Suddenly an older man pushed his way into our conversation, clearly quite irritated with me. He was introduced to me as a local judge working in the family courts. He pointed his finger and started to snarl at me: 'How dare you call these people *victims*,' he barked. 'Only I can decide if they are victims or not, do you hear me? I will decide.'

I was somewhat taken aback; everyone was. To be fair I think the man had had a little too much champagne. We all stood in silence, not sure how to respond, as he was so aggressive. I could feel one of the women organisers digging her fingers into the small of my back, and I took this as a plea not to respond to him. I was shaken. I am absolutely sure that he would not have spoken to me like that if I had been a man.

I was talking with Professor Evan Stark about this issue one day. 'The thing is, Jane,' he observed, 'I can say things you never could, and because I'm a man, I get away with it.' He did not mean he could swear or be outrageous – he was referring to his ability and freedom to professionally challenge others, male or female, without suffering an aggressive attack. This was his experience over the years.

The judge in the marquee eventually stalked off, and the woman said to me: 'We mustn't upset him: this is a fundraiser and we need the money, and some of us will have to face him in the courts next week.' She had been coerced into allowing this man's privileged and aggressive display, and was imploring me to stay quiet too, for me to collude. I did stay quiet – for her. I did not feel comfortable at all with the idea that this man presided over a family court, and I felt it was ironic that such a display should be seen at a fundraiser for domestic abuse. It is not the only or even the worst time I have been verbally attacked by all manner of professionals, male and female, but given the field in which I work, I am always surprised.

As a woman on my own much of the time, I am constantly reminded of the way power and control threads its way through every part of society. I often remember something Frank Mullane, the CEO of AAFDA, whose sister and nephew were murdered, said when we were presenting a masterclass together to a few hundred police officers about coercive control and homicide. He was talking about getting the facts heard, even if that is difficult, and being unafraid to do that. 'I imagine the dead person,' he said, 'standing at my shoulder shouting, *No, that's not how it was!* and I feel a responsibility to let them be heard.' It is important to try and balance the stories, and the victim's voice is crucial in the homicide story, even if it is difficult for some to hear. Loud voices that seek to drown out those that are less powerful, especially if that is through a sense of entitlement, are actually leaving us all less safe.

Most of us, especially women, will try not to put ourselves in the position of having to face aggression. Threat-assessment expert Gavin de Becker states that women have to protect themselves from possible abuse and assault in ways men just do not understand. Women must make decisions about their safety, based on their sex, on a routine and daily basis. The extent of that social conditioning – and the extent of female fear at many different levels – has been articulated in the growing Me Too movement, which has revealed the extent of sexual harassment and aggression that women face. This fear of aggression and social conditioning to be nice can give opportunities for controlling people to push themselves onto others and start to manipulate.

So stage two is not just about speed, it is about speed *and* commitment. Slowing things down, even if that feels difficult, can give a person time to think, time to see how a new partner may respond to challenges. How a potential partner responds to not getting their own way from the get-go, before the relationship moves forward, will be very telling and will give an idea of how they might behave in the future when the stakes may be higher.

Jealousy and possessiveness are actually very selfish character traits when they are excessive and routine, not a sign of a loving and caring person. Relationships with routinely jealous people need careful monitoring. Anyone should be wary of being treated as a possession early on – possession is about ownership of property, not about love. A person in such a situation should step back and put the brakes on while things are still slow enough that there will not be much fallout.

This stage in the timeline has captured the imagination of many professionals, who feel that education about relationships and jealousy, for example, should start in school. Getting in at the earliest stages so that jealousy and possessiveness are perceived as problematic, and not about love, could be a really important challenge to coercive control. There is a difference between love and possession, even if there are some crossovers in the way these things look, and we should all recognise the difference. It might also give people with control issues a chance to identify this as a problem in themselves and make moves to do something about it.

Everyone can be a little jealous sometimes, and this is normal, but patterns of jealousy and attempts to control through it are always a red flag. If we ever accept excessive jealousy and excuse or justify it, we just strengthen the control.

3

Stage Three: Living with control

When I was in school I was the subject of sustained and unpleasant bullying by a group of girls who were older than me. I am not sure why they started; I just know that they stole a good two years of my life, with aftershocks well into my adulthood. The abuse literally hurtled into my consciousness in the form of a bewildering and brutal assault that left more shock than it did injury. In that moment, with my head reeling from a punch, I tried to make sense of what was happening. Also in that moment, my relationship with myself changed: a profound and instant restructuring of my sense of personal safety. Suddenly I knew that I was, quite frankly, pitifully ill-equipped to protect myself. I lost respect for me, and I lost trust in me. I still feel as if I should have risen ninja-like from the floor and trounced my attackers with superhuman phys-ical fighting skills. I truly believe that I would be more of a friend to myself now if I had been capable of that.

Reality and isolation left me to manage the situation and I had to learn quickly. I did not have the power to end the bullying. However, I can report that, for the most part, I was hugely successful in avoiding further physical assaults: I managed the abuse. I had to be hyper-vigilant. I had to plan every minute of my school day; I had to manipulate and manoeuvre where

I would be and when; I had to be constantly aware. I was living in the future, not the present, and it was exhausting.

Those girls controlled every minute of my day from inside my head. I only became free of them when my family relocated and I went to a new school. But the new relationship with safety, and the new relationship with myself – that moved with me.

There are strong parallels here with coercive control. Those girls were able to control every aspect of my life with a mixture of the fear and uncertainty they had instilled in me with that first assault, and with the ongoing campaign to keep reminding me of it. I managed the threat, but it was all-consuming and utterly exhausting.

For many people subject to coercive control, the difficulties and danger signs are not as immediately obvious as a physical assault. Stealth and manipulation open the door for coercive control, and this is made easy because we are not even looking for it. Every risky behaviour has a plausible explanation that encourages us to ignore it. Every method of control is designed to ensure and maintain the compliance of the subject of it. Compliance does not always feel like control at the beginning.

There are two pillars of control that often kick-start every other means by which compliance is maintained in an intimate relationship. I call these the *jealousy code* and the *loyalty code*.

The jealousy code

We have seen how jealousy is often used in a 'crime of passion' narrative as a defence for murder, so it is not surprising that it is also a plausible justification for control. Jealousy is seen as a natural output of romantic love, and that may be true to some extent. Some isolated jealousy may be reasonable and defensible. But patterns of jealousy that are used to try and alter someone's behaviours or choices are not reasonable – ever.

Controlling people often want their partner to avoid doing things that make them jealous – or this is how it will be sold. They may say things like: 'I just can't handle it when I see you talking to other men. It's just because you arouse such strong feelings in me,' or: 'I don't like it when you wear that dress: it's making other men look at you and I just get so jealous.'

Just think about it: how do we ensure we do not make someone jealous? I don't mean on one specific occasion, I mean when in a relationship with a person whose jealousy is a pattern – it is part of who they are. Do we avoid talking to others – the delivery person, the nurse, the teacher, the colleague, the neighbour? Perhaps we should not dress in ways that make us too attractive; maybe we should stop going out without our partner; perhaps we avoid former partners, or even watching films with attractive characters. Maybe we should not have close friendships or talk to people on social media; we should never, ever flirt with anyone or maybe even smile at them; and possibly we should even make our phone available for scrutiny and let our partner have all our passwords. The list of things we could avoid doing might be endless and unknowable.

The jealousy code might actually manoeuvre individuals into living an isolated and miserable life where their freedoms are severely limited. This may be something they are happy to do right at the beginning of a relationship, where they might believe themselves to be in the throes of a great passion. Or it may be something they are willing to accept because they want to impose some rules themselves. After all, they would do all these things if they had got nothing to hide, right? Wrong. It is a simple but powerful ruse to get them to agree to comply with someone else's demands. It reveals a partner's paranoia and entitlement, not their love.

Jealousy is often simultaneously underpinned through the powerful sexual double standard that seeks to control and restrict women's sexuality, sexual expression and sexual behaviours. Excessively jealous people have their feelings of entitlement validated through these social scripts. So pressure to comply with a partner's jealousy is applied on two fronts: through emotional blackmail and through cultural conventions.

Young people in their first relationships are particularly vulnerable to seeing excessive jealousy as a sign of great love. When a boyfriend turns up somewhere unannounced it is because they were worrying, or they just had to see you. When a girlfriend gets angry because you spoke to an ex, they say it is because you arouse such strong feelings, and so it goes on. It can seem flattering at first, but the control that the jealousy code brings rises as surely and as unstoppably as the tide.

Excessive or persistent jealousy is always a warning sign, because excessive jealousy reflects a behavioural pattern, a way of thinking, a constant threat. The control and manipulation that jealousy forgives brings us much closer to understanding how coercive control can take hold of a life and condense it to a mere shadow of what it once was. The jealousy code and the myth of the crime of passion give power to controlling people because they have become plausible explanations for what is actually *control*. The loyalty code often follows quickly on the heels of the jealousy code, and completes an effective circle of control within which other controls are cultivated.

The loyalty code

The loyalty code is imposed through a series of hidden tests designed to make someone choose between two sides and prove their devotion to the controlling person. It is an effective method to remove or control the influence others may have over the victim. Very often friends and family will be the focus. Friends may be considered 'a bad influence' and family may be described as 'trying to split up' the relationship. The victim may be manipulated to see less of their friends or family, or be responsible for making sure they 'like' the controlling person or at least act as if they do. It is a very common part of coercive control that victims are required to present a happy face to others; it is a loyalty test. If outsiders become suspicious, or the controlling person is criticised, there will be consequences for the victim. A happy front can be a protective factor, but it increases the control and the things that support that control.

More socially confident controlling people may keep family members close so that they can be monitored and even used to help control the victim. Family members may come to see the controlling person as loving and capable, and question any criticism the victim may raise. This is purposeful.

*

Sada

Both the jealousy and the loyalty codes were used with paralysing effect on a young woman called Sada. I tell her story using her own words to show how insidious, but effective, these two pillars can be.

Sada's dad emailed me late one night. We did not know each other, but he was desperate. He had seen me talking on the television about coercive control murders and he felt I was his last hope. Sada had died quite unexpectedly one morning with her packed bags around her. She was planning to leave her husband. Sada's parents were convinced her death was suspicious, but no one was listening to them.

We vastly underestimate the true number of murders, and it can be very difficult to convince police, coroners and others that a death is suspicious if they have made up their minds it is not. I agreed to meet with Sada's family to listen to their concerns.

Sada had started to do things that her parents did not understand; they knew something was wrong and they knew when it had started, but they did not know why. Sada loved her family and they had always been close, so it was strange that she ignored them when they visited one day – staying in the bedroom with her husband while they played with the children in the living room. Sada loved the idea of big families and glorious weddings, so it was alarming when she did not invite her family to her own wedding and her nieces were not bridesmaids, as she had always promised they would be. She had always spent at least two or three days a week with her sisters, so it was strange when she just stopped coming round. Everyone knew she had changed since she met Rohan, and they knew something was not right.

Sada kept diaries – secret diaries. After her death her father found them. I was allowed to read them and realised straight away that Sada was living with coercive control. A random page from those diaries reads: 'This morning my beautiful boy gave me a wonderful smile. My beautiful Samar! I decided we would go out today, it was so sunny, just me and Samar. We left about 11.00 and on the way to the park he fell asleep, bless his little heart.'

I got a feel for the person Sada was: a caring young woman, doing ordinary, everyday things, and feeling ordinary, everyday emotions. The next line read: 'We went into the park and fed the ducks. Then Rohan rang, it all turned and I got anxious again, I just sat on the bench and cried. Poor Samar, he has a terrible mummy.'

There was no explanation as to why the conversation 'turned', why she started to cry, or why she thought she was a bad mother.

Sada was in her early twenties when she met Rohan. They had moved in together quickly and Samar was born within the year. Rohan was attentive and romantic at the beginning, and Sada was enthralled. According to her diary he would say things like, 'I'm just a jealous guy,' and 'It makes my blood boil when I see another man moving in on you.' And Sada said she understood.

He said I can't help it, you arouse these feelings in me. He always says that when he's been angry. He loses his temper and shouts right in my face. He broke my phone on Tuesday when he chucked it, then he just said I'm sorry I don't mean to frighten you, I just love you so much. I don't mean to make him mad, but he can't help it if he's just like that. I need to do better.

Rohan imposed the jealousy code straight away; it justified and explained his frightening behaviours, obscuring their threat. Sada thought his explanation was feasible, so she quietly consented to changing her behaviour. Rohan spent so much time with her in those early days that she did not really notice how entwined their lives had become and that she only seemed to spend time with him.

It did seem sensible that they live together, and so without much planning or forethought they were sharing a house within weeks, and as a family less than a year later. Arguments with Rohan soon became a regular occurrence and Sada found that she always seemed to be breaking the jealousy code somehow. She would wear the wrong thing, or talk to the wrong people. It was impossible to know what might make Rohan jealous. She said she felt she was walking on eggshells. 'I was in my blue summer dress and sandals,' she confided to her diary.

He had complained about me in that dress before, so I changed it for my red one. But I knew he'd say something about that too. I just didn't know what to wear to please him, he always makes some comment. I tried three dresses but none were right. I started to get all hot and crying. All that stress because I was scared about what he would say. I tried so hard to get it right but he just made a nasty comment anyway. I wish I knew how to please him, I can't take much more.

Every time Rohan got angry, Sada would try to fix things. Even if she stood her ground, which she regularly did in the early days, it made her feel she was either blocking a resolution to the problem or making things worse. She felt responsible and Rohan encouraged her to feel that way. She knew the consequences of upsetting him, so Sada did what many girls would do in her situation – she confided in her mother.

I told my mum I'm messing it up, I'm always being really dumb and doing stupid stuff to spoil things, I make him angry. I wish I was better. Mum said you need to get shot of him, she said it won't get any better you know, it'll just get worse.

Back at home Rohan had decided Sada's mother had too much influence.

He says my mum hates him, he says she's always giving me that look that makes him feel like a criminal in his own home, he says he thinks she's trying to split us up and that I always take her side. I don't take her side, I told him, she's my mum, that's all.

Sada was stuck in the middle. She wanted to confide in her mum; she wanted to be able to vent about Rohan. But he was right: her mum did not like him.

Rohan kept piling on the pressure at home.

'He said I can tell when you've seen her because you change. He says when I've seen her I'm different and then he said I'm just like her. He won't let it drop. It's really upsetting me.'

This was Rohan imposing the loyalty code. Sada was being manipulated into choosing between Rohan and her mother. 'I'll go and see my mum,' she wrote in her diary, 'but I won't tell him, or do it when he's around. It's probably best just to keep them apart.'

As I read Sada's words, I could see with increasing gloom that Rohan was controlling. The next entry showed her relationship tipping predictably, from bad to dangerous:

Rohan started shouting at me, he was making out that everything is all my fault. He says I'm making him miserable because I'm not right in the head, he says I'm unstable. I told him that he always blames me for everything. He said I'd never been right in the head. I wish we could be like a team again, like the beginning, and I'm trying to make changes. He said he's taking me to the doctor to get me looked at.

There is a term – gaslighting – that refers to a pattern of behaviour designed to make victims of control feel that they are unstable. It comes from the 1938 play and the later film *Gaslight*, which tells the story of a man manipulating his wife into believing she is going insane.

Gaslighting generally works by making victims unable to trust their own perceptions and instincts, and they can become afraid to make decisions without help. Very often women's menstrual cycles will be used to underpin gaslighting tactics: I found to my dismay that Rohan had started keeping a calendar on the wall in the kitchen with the predicted dates of Sada's periods. 'I agreed with him, I'm unstable and weak,' Sada wrote in her diary. 'I think I'm going crazy. He knows when it's my time of the month. I'm starting to dread it, I feel things getting on top of me and it's not fair to him or anyone.'

Sada recognised that she was trapped in a toxic cycle with Rohan, where she was conflicted and distressed: she wrote a note to him in her secret diary, saying what she felt she could not say to his face:

Rohan you are so cruel and domineering. You always have to be right. I wish you wouldn't talk to me like I am stupid. You don't know what it's like looking after a baby and how tired I get. You think you know everything and how I should act and how I should do things . . . I don't want to upset you and break up our family. I'm trying so hard, I felt we used to be like a team, us against the world, but now I just feel so lonely. It's over, I'm leaving.

She then decided to tell him to his face how she felt:

> He was so angry, it got really frightening. He said he'd had enough and he was leaving. He packed his bags, there was nothing I could say. I don't see how our marriage is going to work after this. We are right at the end I think. He walked out, took his bags and he slammed the door. About half an hour after he just came back with a huge bunch of flowers, he was so upset. I could see tears in his eyes. I think it broke his heart.

Sada felt that Rohan was devastated by her strong stance, and forgot completely how distressed she had been. She felt guilty for 'breaking him'. Rohan consolidated his transformation in suddenly proposing marriage to Sada. She was euphoric, and the hope that things would change dominated her thinking; all thoughts of splitting up were gone. She started to plan the wedding. But there was a price to pay for the proposal, and the loyalty code was used to devastating effect: 'He said, your mother and your sisters, they just hate me. It'll spoil the day if they're there. You know what they're like, they'll just say the wrong thing and they'll just make me feel bad. It's my day too and they will spoil it.'

It is not unusual for the victim's family to be denigrated or undermined, so that the controlling person's perspective and their values appear superior. 'Rohan doesn't want mum at the wedding,' she wrote. 'I don't blame him because she doesn't like him. I don't want the day spoiled, not after he's made such an effort. He said we'll have a second wedding when we've got more money. This will just be a quick one, just to show me he loves me and we're a team together.'

Sada told her family in the kindest way that it was to be a very small wedding and there would be no guests; however, there would be a second celebration later, which they would be invited to.

Of course this never happened. Rohan's family attended the wedding. This sent a clear message to Sada's family that Rohan was in charge, which pleased him greatly. Rohan had now effectively isolated Sada from anyone he had no control or influence over. He was now the single biggest presence in her life.

Rohan needed to assure himself that Sada was obeying his rules, even when he was not there. Sada told of constant texting and calling throughout the day; she said he was always calling to 'check she was okay':

Rohan rung again about 11 again checking I was ok, but he started getting all angry about the dishes. He says that he's working all day and I'm just sitting around being lazy. He says it's not fair and I should be trying harder to be a good mother and wife.

I saw a great buggy on gumtree. I arranged with the woman to go and pick it up after Rohan gets home. I started to panic, I should have asked him first. I got really worried thinking about what he'd say. I just cancelled the whole thing, I shouldn't have just decided like that. When I told him about it, he said I should've just gone and got it, he wouldn't have minded! I am so stupid.

Nothing in Sada's diaries suggested she was doing anything challenging or hurtful, so she should never have had to fear the repercussions of making a decision to buy a second-hand pushchair. These were ordinary everyday behaviours that did not even break the jealousy or the loyalty codes. But things had gone much further than that: Sada's liberties and status had been eroded and her world was now much smaller.

By this time Sada was controlling her own behaviour: Rohan did not even need to be there. Just the knowledge that he could be nasty and threatening meant she constantly tried to keep things calm. She wrote:

> I feel miserable and upset all the time, I just seem to cry for no reason, and getting up is getting harder. I can't tell Rohan – he thinks I'm just moaning. I sneaked a half-hour sleep on the sofa today, I hope he doesn't find out. I saw the doctor and I told her I was scared of Rohan, but I begged her not to put that in my records. I couldn't have him finding out. I shouldn't really have said anything.

In the late eighteenth century the social reformer and philosopher Jeremy Bentham designed a prison called a panopticon. It was a new idea and consisted of a large circular building with lots of cells with windows. There was a central guard's tower that did not have clear windows. The guards could see the prisoners, but the prisoners could not see the guards. The idea was that because the prisoners never knew when they were being watched, they would self-regulate: they would always behave, just in case they were being watched. This is what happens with coercive control: chronic fear keeps victims managing their behaviour, even if the controlling person is not there.

Sada became pregnant again and lost financial and physical power. 'I don't like that midwife,' Rohan would say. 'She's trying to tell you what to do. You don't have to listen to her; she doesn't know you like I do.' He had little patience with the difficulties of pregnancy but simultaneously felt the benefits of Sada's increasing vulnerability. It was all worth it, though, because now he had got a lifelong lever that would maintain his control for ever. These were his babies.

Sada gave birth not long before Christmas and was dependent on Rohan to help her buy presents. She was asking, and then begging him, to take her to buy presents, and he kept letting her down. He left it to the very last minute to take her shopping, and then tightly controlled what she was allowed to spend. Sada was very distressed on Christmas Day, when she felt she had so little for her children. She said it nearly broke her:

> I had hardly anything for Samar, I cried and cried. Mum and Dad came round on Christmas Day. I honestly didn't know they were coming. He was so mad about it, he said I knew and I had hidden it from him. He wouldn't come out of the bedroom, he just stayed in there. I didn't know what to do. I wished they would just go, there was going to be trouble, I just wanted to get it over with. I left Mum with the kids and I sat with him in the bedroom, just trying to keep things calm.

Rohan was also pressurising Sada to be involved in sexual behaviours she was uncomfortable with. 'I don't want to do what he likes . . . it's got so bad I can't bear him even to touch me now,' she told her diary. 'I never really liked it before, it feels just wrong, especially after I had my baby. I told him but he pushed me to do it anyway. Now even talking about it feels disgusting.' Sada describes things getting more menacing:

He was just sitting there on the sofa one day, he had no trousers on and he had a hard-on. He was just sitting there, he never said anything, he just sat there like that not saying anything. I didn't say anything either, I didn't know what to do. I just hate him so much now…

Finally, Sada decided to just cut the ties and leave Rohan, whatever the consequences. She packed all her bags. She piled them in the bedroom and told him of her plan to leave with the children the following morning.

Hours later Sada was dead in the bedroom, surrounded by her packed bags. The paramedics were told by Rohan that it was an accident. The cause of Sada's death was never definitively established. The police have their suspicions; we worked together to explore the possibility of a prosecution, but gathering evidence was ultimately too difficult.

*

People who are witness to controlling behaviours do not always know the importance of what they have seen. We are all programmed to look for signs of violence but maybe cannot imagine that control lurks hidden, and is very often underpinned by low-level assaults and threats. The way victims behave in the face of fear is sometimes confusing, but can be quite logical if seen through the lens of coercive control.

Controlling people will attempt to trap victims in the relationship, making it impossible for them to leave. This has been described by Professor Evan Stark as being like a hostage situation. Victims can spend a lot of time trying to convince partners that they are devoted and loyal, because this can help keep things calm or safer.

The twentieth-century American author and philosopher Eric Hoffer once said: 'You can discover what your enemy fears most by observing the means he uses to frighten you.' Coercive control is frequently driven by the fears of its perpetrators, and maintained by the fears of its victims. Perpetrators often fear losing what makes them feel stable, or losing what they feel entitled to. These are two different but related fears. To fear losing something that gives you stability might be quite easy to understand, but losing something you think you are entitled to is about an attack on your status and your sense of justice. It can be humiliating or shameful to lose status or what you perceive of as rights. Some feel enraged by this.

These feelings of entitlement may come in part from narcissistic tendencies, or self-centred views of the world, but equally they are intertwined with cultural belief systems that may put people in hierarchies and designate status. Up until 1828 in England and Wales, for example, there was a common law offence known as 'petty treason', and this was an offence committed against a 'superior' by a 'subordinate' – for example, a servant killing a master. It legally inscribed hierarchy, and in cases of homicide a woman would be charged with petty treason rather than murder for killing or attempting to kill a husband; a husband killing a wife would be charged with the lesser offence of murder. The purpose of this law was to ensure people remained in their place, a significant social imperative at the time, especially where class and status were so important.

Controlling people often believe that a partner and any children belong to them and are more likely to see separation as an attack on their ego and their rights. They can see the world as a series of hierarchies, and they are always above their partner and children. They often fear humiliation more keenly than physical threats, which gives us some insight into their world.

Fear is complex, but we tend to think of it in very simple terms. If we can think of two different but related types of fear, the ways in which victims behave and respond to coercive control may become clearer.

Fear

Gavin de Becker argues that we all have intuition that alerts us to threats to our safety. He calls it *the gift of fear*. Fear is quite a complex physical response that all normal humans experience, and it is a survival mechanism. It is regulated by a part of the brain called the amygdala which, when activated, temporarily takes over our conscious thoughts. When we perceive a threat, the amygdala is the first to react and activates what we call our *fight or flight* response. In just a fraction of a second, multiple physical energies are activated that concentrate us on the threat. Our heart rate and breathing will increase, blood is rushed to our muscles to give us help in running or fighting, our pupils dilate so we have more light in our eyes, we are flooded with adrenaline to keep us alert, and cortisol release thickens our blood in case of injury. We can experience auditory exclusion (or relative deafness), tunnel vision, and loss of bladder control. All this and more happens largely without our conscious input. Once the threat is neutralised the brain will release neurotransmitters and hormones that will reverse these changes. There is a sense of relief and things can return to normal.

This *immediate fear* response is often easy to recognise and understand. We would probably try to help someone displaying such signs; we would be concerned. But that is not the only type of fear, and those are not the only signs someone is fearful.

What is often referred to as *chronic fear* is quite different. It is much more difficult to recognise because, for the individual, it is more about trying to predict and avoid harm than responding to a threat that is obviously actually happening. Very like the fear I described when talking about the girls who persecuted me in school.

Chronic fear is incrementally built through experience. Victims learn what provokes the controlling person, and how they respond. Professor Evan Stark says that controlling people will 'instil in the minds of their victims the price of their resistance'. The young woman who would not get in the ambulance had experience of what the price was, or might be, of taking help, so she refused to get in the ambulance. Victims learn quite quickly what happens if they resist the control or upset their partners. Sada was fearful of Rohan, but her fear was shown in the way she avoided anything that might upset or annoy him: she avoided doing things she liked, she avoided dressing how she liked, she even avoided having her family at her own wedding. She believed she was going crazy and that frightened her too. Many people believed that Sada disliked her family, but there is a possibility that Rohan felt better and was more calm when she took his side and maligned her relatives. For this reason, public statements from someone being controlled are not always a reflection of the truth.

So for me, coercive control is both the motivation and the abuse. The motivation is in the controlling person – it is that need to have control and power over their partner's life, enforcing compliance. The abuse is the limits this places on the partner and their ability to do what they want, but also the fear they live with, of the consequences of upsetting the controlling person.

Victim strategies – Lara

Lara is an interesting woman who survived a deadly assault. I met her after her short-term boyfriend, Chris, had been jailed for that assault.

Lara is a young woman in her late twenties. She lives in her own home with two young children. She has a wide circle of friends and her community is small and tight. Chris was part of that community and they both lived in the same area, used the same pubs, and had shared friends. He was very drawn to Lara and began flirting with her and showing that he was interested in a relationship. He was over-attentive and pushy, but this just looked like enthusiasm to Lara's friends. He was a good-looking and friendly guy, but Lara was not interested and resisted his attentions. 'He just kept on and on,' Lara explained. 'It wasn't that he was creepy or anything, and he was actually quite funny, but I wasn't interested. He wasn't my type.'

Lara kept kindly telling Chris she was not interested, but he did not stop. He persisted.

'Everyone knew,' Lara told me. 'He told everyone how much he liked me. Everyone thought it was really sweet, and then they all got involved trying to convince me to go out with him. They were saying like: he's a lovely bloke, you should give it a try, he's so nice.'

Chris started turning up at Lara's house with shared friends. He would sit and have coffee and talk to her children. Then he started turning up on his own, just for a chat.

As things went on, and the pressure from everyone grew, and Chris seemed quite nice, Lara agreed to go out with him. 'We went out a few times and we were seeing each other for a few weeks, but he's just not my type, so I ended it.'

Chris did not accept that the relationship was over, and even Lara's friends kept trying to convince her to give it another go. Lara was firm that she did not want to go out with him. Chris called at her house a few times, again just for a chat, and she gently reaffirmed that she did not want to be a couple any more. He seemed friendly, but Lara was getting concerned that he just would not go away.

'Everything changed one night when he called at the house really late,' she recalls. 'It was dark outside, the kids were in bed and I heard this banging on the door. I saw it was him. I opened the door to tell him to go away, he was making a hell of a noise. I had no reason to be particularly fearful and I didn't want him frightening the children. He pushed past me into the house, and he raped me.'

Everything did indeed change for Lara that evening. She did not scream; she froze. She was terrified that her children would come downstairs. She had few injuries, and she had opened the door to him. Everyone thought he was a lovely bloke. Lara did not think she could go to the police. She did not even think she could tell her friends.

Chris left and she did not see him again for a couple of weeks. But she stopped going to places he might be, she tried to avoid him, and she was now absolutely terrified.

He turned up again one night, banging on Lara's door. This time she did not open the door but called the police. The police told Chris to move on. He told them it was just that he wanted to see his ex. They seemed to understand, and very quickly the incident was over. But Chris came back after they left, banging on the door again and shouting. He did not care about the police; he could easily explain he was a love-struck ex. They might move him on, but nothing more.

'I was terrified now. I knew he wasn't going to leave me alone. I knew he didn't care about the police. I was so worried my kids would be frightened by him. I had to protect them from this – they're just little,' remembered Lara. 'Then the phone calls started. He would just keep on and on calling, sometimes hundreds of calls. I worked out that if I answered him and spoke to him, even if it was only brief, then he would stop for a couple of days. I even worked out the number of times I could ignore the calls before he turned up at the door: it was about nineteen calls. If I answered around then, he wouldn't come to the door.'

Chris would still sometimes turn up late at night, hammering on the door, demanding to be let in, frightening the children. The police did not always get there quickly.

I have viewed CCTV footage of Chris banging on Lara's door in the middle of the night, shouting and yelling, even kicking the door. Lara thought that, just like the phone calls, if she opened the door he might go away. This was a high-stakes move for Lara, but the aggression was rising, the contact was relentless, and her children needed protecting.

What do you do with someone who isn't afraid of the police? Someone who can convince the police he is a nice guy? Lara started to comply with his demands in order to buy herself safety.

Very quickly she learned that if *she allowed Chris to rape her* (and those are her words) then she would buy herself around three weeks' peace. This was not a man who was under any illusion that Lara wanted his attention. He was a man who was enjoying his power over her.

Lara was trapped in a cycle. She had been letting him into her house and answering his calls. Lara was not a quiet or submissive person, so her friends, and his friends, thought they just had an on/off relationship. The reality was so very different. Lara did manage to keep herself safe through this compliance. But the strain and the fear was taking its toll.

Lara decided to try her luck with the police again. She managed to get a restraining order against Chris. Her friends became very critical of her, accusing her of leading him on. Chris did not take the restraining order well either.

One night when Lara was alone and her children were staying with their father, Chris broke into her house. He dragged her up to her bedroom and shut her in with him. He was absolutely livid. Over the next four hours he beat and raped Lara, broke her ribs, tore open the skin on her face, punctured her lung, pulled out her hair, and strangled her to unconsciousness.

As it started to get light outside Chris decided he was going to change location and take Lara somewhere else. Lara's intuition told her he intended to kill her, that the beating was over. It was a miracle that during his attempt to get her in his car she was able to run naked across the street and get the attention of a neighbour, who took her in. Lara was taken to hospital and placed in intensive care.

When the news broke that Chris had been arrested for the assault on Lara, there was widespread shock – and a somewhat mixed response. Some people were horrified on Lara's behalf. However, some felt sorry for Chris and claimed that he was just a man who had snapped under unbearable pressure, a victim of his own jealousy and Lara's mixed signals.

But Lara was being controlled, and in managing her safety in the best way she could, people interpreted that as recklessness. It was the opposite of reckless. In her mind the only way to stop Chris was to comply with his demands, and this managed her safety for a while. When she stopped complying is when Chris became more dangerous.

With the injuries he inflicted she should be dead, but a brief break in the chain of events allowed her to escape and a spell in intensive care saved her life. Lara is not here because Chris was finished with beating her that day; she is here because she escaped before he could kill her. There is a big difference. Chris was prosecuted for assault and sentenced to a prison term.

*

All of this was happening in front of people. Chris managed to get compliance, and that compliance did not look like fear; it looked like consent.

Bonnie had the same experience with Karl. She had to let Karl back into her life to keep herself safe from the consequences of refusing him access. For Bonnie, it was not her friends who did not understand her concerns and fears – for her it was the police. She went to the police and reported

Karl on many occasions. The police would turn up and tell Karl to go away and calm down. They could not understand why, just two weeks later, there would be another call from Bonnie asking for help in identical circumstances.

It is the consequences for victims that need to be managed. If someone is frightened, say, and we, be it as a friend or as a professional, wanted to make suggestions to them about their safety, we could say to them: 'What are the consequences likely to be of this?' If the advice was to change the locks on their doors, ask them what the consequences of this would be for them: will the person just try to kick the door in? Are they likely to just accept the changed locks? Will there be something else worrying that happens in response? I could have said to the woman who would not get in the ambulance: 'What are the likely consequences for you if you get in that ambulance?' Or: 'How can we help you manage that?' But I did not have that understanding of abuse back then.

When I spoke with the police about Bonnie, after she was killed, an officer told me that 'Bonnie would not stay away from Karl' – she kept going back to him. I suggested that perhaps *he* would not leave *her* alone, or that she was unable to shake him off. Or perhaps going back was safer? Much like my first sergeant all those years ago, the police officer could not understand the behaviour of the victim. Calls for help were treated as if Bonnie and Karl had had a bit of an argument – one as bad as the other: a gross misjudgement of what was going on.

*

My first real experience of extreme violence directed against me happened one evening in a petrol station. I was with two friends, and as we got out of the car we saw a group of young men attacking the attendant on the forecourt. The attendant ran into the shop and locked the doors behind him, leaving a group of around four or five young men outside. They looked as if they were going to try and continue the attack. I went to the forecourt emergency phone and called the police. As I was talking to the control room, the men approached me and told me to put the phone down. I continued with the call until, suddenly, I was punched in the face. Then the whole group of young men started to punch and hit me and my friends.

Every time I was hit and knocked to the floor I just kept getting up; I remember getting up and falling down, completely disorientated, a number of times. Somehow it seemed safer to be on my feet. It went on for what seemed like ages. I did not have the strength or the skill to involve myself in a fight with this gang of men, and I knew the police were on their way. My friends and I were battered and bruised when the men finally ran at the sound of the sirens. It was the first time I had been repeatedly punched in the head and face with such determination and force. The experience was terrifying. We were all lucky not to have had more serious injuries.

Some of the men were arrested some time later. The trial was a traumatic experience in itself, as the men had a barrister each and we were cross-examined ruthlessly by them. Eventually they were found guilty and were each sentenced to a prison term.

Now this experience is different in many ways from that of a victim of domestic violence. First, I did not know my attackers and that distance made giving evidence a more straightforward process. Second, as a victim of a stranger attack, I was viewed in a sympathetic light by the jury and the judge. This does not always happen in cases of domestic abuse, where victims are often assessed for their 'culpability'. Also, I did not have to go back home to my attacker or shield my child from the violence.

I do think that the justice system was designed to deal with *incidents* rather than *patterns*, and this is one of the problems. Evidence gathering for patterns (both coercive control and stalking are patterns) is very different from evidence gathering after an incident. The courts are also not designed to take full account of power differentials between parties. They put victims and offenders side by side in court, and though there are special measures designed to address being face to face with an offender, the whole process requires the victim to engage in an adversarial battle with a person they are afraid of, or who has power over them.

The processes to address witness intimidation are not as developed as they could or should be. The adversarial system requires that people engage with each other as combatants, and, by their very nature, stalking and coercive control stack the odds against victims. The victims of these offences are motivated to escape the abuse and to get the patterns to stop – not to get into a war with their abuser and escalate things: that is what they are desperately trying to avoid.

In stark contrast, people who divide the world into winners and losers, and are comfortable with, or even enjoy, combat, are less intimidated. It is their terms in the courtroom, legitimised and perpetuated. Many of the assumptions made about the adversarial system are flawed, and those who know the system well, like Sir Keir Starmer, for example, when he was the Director of Public Prosecutions, have questioned how effective it is.

Simone

Simone had lived a seemingly idyllic life: married to Henri for over thirty years, living in a beautiful house in a lovely location with no money worries, their children grown up, and with healthy, happy grandchildren. But what seems perfect rarely is.

I was meeting Simone in hospital and I could see from her notes that coercive control had dominated her life. A control that had blended seamlessly into the marriage, no longer questioned, no longer resisted. It was the twine that bound her and Henri, a tightly wound and tangled knot, impossible to unravel after so many years.

I had driven some miles to see her and it was a ferociously sunny day. I gratefully climbed from my car and stood for a minute in the gentle breeze just to look at the hospital gardens. The hospital was pristine and well managed, and though I cannot remember which magazines were neatly piled on the tables, I think that *Country Life* would not have been out of place. It was a reminder that anyone could be affected by coercive control – irrespective of class, age, ethnicity or education. Irrespective of everything.

A self-assured voice announced the presence of a tall, slim woman with beautifully styled deep-brown hair; she was aged around fifty, and was striding purposefully towards me. I could see another woman behind her, less commanding, much quieter and more reserved. I think she was of similar age, but couldn't have been more different; her hair was greying and far more casual. She was rushing a little to keep up with the woman in front, who threw out her hand to me and stated: 'You must be Jane. Lovely to meet you – come this way.' The other woman smiled and we all entered a café area to sit and talk.

I had not met Simone before, and I was intrigued to hear her story. So, as we sat down and the confident woman strode off to get coffee, I thanked her for agreeing to speak with me: 'Oh, I'm not Simone,' she said, smiling. 'That's Simone getting the coffee.'

We both turned to look at Simone, who was striding back with a tray of coffees. I just assumed, because Simone was so self-assured and in charge, that she was there to support and look after the other woman.

Simone sat down opposite me on a pastel-coloured armchair, arranging the soft cushions around her, and spent the next two hours telling me all about the life she had planned for herself when she left hospital. 'I have it all sorted out, and I can't wait,' she explained. 'It's going to be a whole new life.' She had managed to buy a property back in her native France which she wanted to run as a restaurant and had employed a local couple to look after it while she was in hospital. Simone appeared genuinely enthused and happy. She was looking forward to starting her new life and she was excited to talk about it. I had to encourage her to talk to me about what happened in the days and weeks before she killed Henri.

Women make up only around 10 per cent of homicide perpetrators. Women who kill their husbands or partners are a smaller proportion of that, and women who kill their partners because they planned to, and not in retaliation for domestic abuse, are a proportion of that. So the numbers are much lower than male killers. However, even though women like Simone are not as common, they do exist, and they show similar patterns to people like Karl and Vincent. They are often controlling and self-focused, and feel more outrage than love when they are rejected.

Twenty-five-year-old Hasna Begum is a good example. She killed her former partner Pietro Sanna in June 2017, stabbing him thirty-six times in a planned and frenzied attack, taking him completely by surprise. Begum, who was only four feet eleven and physically small, said she had been defending herself when she killed Pietro. The jury disbelieved her, and she was found guilty of murder and sentenced to life, with a tariff of twenty years.

Simone's husband Henri had been a professional man who owned several restaurants. He was widely liked and respected in his community; from everything that everyone said, he was a kind and generous person. Simone was not liked as much and seemed to have lots of arguments and confrontations with people, including her colleagues and her family. She was certainly very forceful – the way she completely dominated the guard who accompanied her in this secure hospital was quite fascinating. I could imagine that she might easily challenge people and become very difficult to manage.

She spoke to me about a dispute she had had with her husband's colleagues at a restaurant she had taken an interest in and this revealed a recurring theme throughout our discussions that day. 'I was treated badly,' she said of her husband's colleagues. 'I had some fabulous plans for the menu and the decor, and they just couldn't see my vision. I know what I'm talking about and they didn't like it. We owned the place, after all.' In reality, Simone had not had much to do with Henri's businesses, but suddenly decided she wanted to be involved, or, more importantly, in charge.

Her tone throughout was indignant, as if she felt she had been the subject of some sort of injustice. Like many people who kill their spouses, Simone had an unwavering belief in her own entitlement, and seemed to feel that there had been an outrageous failure to ensure she had everything that was due to her. In Simone's world, there are strict hierarchies, and she sits at the top of most of them. Despite her domineering personality, I found her to be thin-skinned. She would see criticism where there was none and challenge it every time. I could easily imagine that living with her would take a lot of management. 'If only they'd listened to me,' she continued. 'They had no idea what they were doing. I told them, and I was proved right.'

This was Simone talking to me about an unrelated social event that had happened some years before at another restaurant involving different people – she had veered off on a seemingly irrelevant memory. But there was a relevant link, and that was people who challenged her. This event was still on her mind: her orders had not been followed and she could not let it go; her annoyance was palpable. She had kept this grudge for a very long time and even felt it appropriate to bring it up during an interview about why she had killed her husband.

This is one of the reasons I do not try to guide conversations with controlling people. It is more instructive to let them show me what is important to them, what really drives them. Simone was showing me that petty arguments and perceived injustices filled her head, no matter what the context of the conversation.

It is not surprising, then, to hear that she had lots of arguments with nearly everyone. Those who could manage her, and avoid upsetting her, would possibly be able to get along with her, like Henri. His life had seemed to revolve around managing his wife's expectations. When she got into the dispute with his staff, something that wasn't really any of her business, it was a big event, because she was being challenged, she wasn't getting her own way, and she didn't like it. She wanted Henri to stand up for her and show solidarity with her position. She wanted Henri to fire all of the people at the restaurant to punish them. But Henri wanted her to back down, probably because he felt she was in the wrong. This insufferable act of disloyalty, as she saw it, was to define the rest of their marriage.

She started to obsess about Henri's perceived disloyalty, and the suspicion that he might leave her followed quite quickly. This put in motion a campaign of stalking and control that overshadowed Henri's life; she would text him all day long when he was at work, demanding his attention and his immediate response; she would go through his things, paranoid that he was unfaithful; she would rifle through his pockets and check his phone and internet activity so she knew all his business; she began to threaten suicide, and Henri was forced to worry about her safety. She began turning up to his restaurants, making verbal threats to his colleagues. The police were called more than once. Everyone thought she was having some sort of breakdown.

It was clear to all who knew them that Henri was having difficulties with Simone. Most people, including Henri, only saw the danger she presented to herself and missed the growing danger to him. When Simone killed Henri it was planned and callous. She stabbed him multiple times in the restaurant kitchen after closing. Afterwards she called the police, claiming she had no memory of what happened and had suffered a blackout. Because Simone had a very visible and documented history of unpredictable behaviour and threats to kill herself, she was assessed as unable to plead. She did not deny killing Henri and was given a hospital order. This is an alternative to a prison sentence for those deemed to require treatment for their mental health.

Simone did not want to talk to me about Henri: it seemed as though she had moved on from that part of her life, focusing on her new life and what that would be when she left the hospital. She told me she would be able to convince the medical professionals that she was well enough to be released within the next twelve to eighteen months. I believed her capable of this, and that sent a shiver down my spine.

Henri lived with fear, but he was not cowering in a corner warding off violent blows, as some of the other victims I've described had done repeatedly over time. His fear was complex, and evidenced in his compliance with Simone's demands. He was fearful of provoking her anxieties and largely tried to manage their lives so that Simone was placated. He tried very hard to cope with what he thought was psychiatric illness. Looking at Simone's history, she had always been controlling and difficult. It was a pattern. Even where there may be mental illness, a history of control is relevant.

My meeting with Simone was certainly thought-provoking and again, although there are clear differences between Vincent, Karl and Simone, for me, their similarities are the most compelling part. All three were individuals who felt a need, a sense of entitlement, to control their partners; they saw it as a non-negotiable part of their intimate relationships. They were all responding to a breakdown of their control – whether it was real, threatened or suspected – when they killed their partners. They all found the breakdown in control to be absolutely intolerable. Though their victims were quite different, all were manipulated into compliance. The victims prioritised the needs of their controlling partners at the expense of their own; all were fearful of the consequences of upsetting them. All victims experienced the fear and manipulation differently, but all responded to it in very similar ways – through compliance. From these seemingly very different cases, it is clear that controlling people are not all the same. But there are links and similarities, and it is these that we should not ignore.

Men in gay relationships, for instance, are at a higher risk of intimate homicide than most men. They may often have more complex aspects to their lives that can make coercive control very powerful, such as not always wanting or feeling able to be open about their sexuality, making them vulnerable to threats. Also people from many communities that are marginalised in some way may find the threat of isolation particularly damaging.

I came to hear of the case of a young man who was in a relationship with an older man through the homicide review that was being conducted. It has been found that where there is a large age difference in a relationship, irrespective of sex, and the older person is controlling, the risk of harm is higher. The younger man was less experienced in the ways of the world than his older partner, and he had a drug misuse problem.

His partner knew this and used his problems to gain control over him; he encouraged, provided and paid for illicit drugs for him. The young man finally decided, with the help of his friends, that he would leave the relationship, as he found the control too much to live with. However, on the day of the separation, the young man suffered a catastrophic overdose of illicit drugs provided to him by the older partner.

Sometimes, when there are drugs involved in the death of a person, this can cloud the issues, and coercive control becomes less visible, the drugs acting almost like a smoking gun, diverting attention and giving easy but incorrect answers. Most cases will be complex, but because someone has alcohol or drug problems, or mental health problems, this does not mean they are not controlled. In fact, drugs and alcohol increase the potential for control, and can be administered by controlling people, or the drug user can be encouraged to take them. They can also be used as self-medication. Mental health vulnerabilities can also be used to undermine someone's claims of abuse. These things make the person easier to control and easier to doubt.

Simone had always been paranoid that Henri would leave her, and that thought increasingly dominated her thinking. She used her own mental health to control him. She would constantly accuse him of wanting to leave; she would accuse him of being involved with other women, women they knew. She would routinely check his phone for evidence and accuse him of plotting behind her back; she would stage suicide attempts and make sure all focus was on her. The threat of separation was in Simone's head, but she did not feel sadness that Henri might leave her: like many controlling people, she felt indignation, outrage and resentment.

I have spoken about the jealousy code and the loyalty code, which can introduce and maintain control, and also gaslighting, which can weaken resistance. Often interwoven into stage three is another clear pattern – the application of *routine and ritual*.

Routine and ritual

If you want to see a poignant sketch on the workings of routine and ritual just watch Pauline Collins and Bernard Hill talking about 'chips and egg' in the film *Shirley Valentine* (1989). The eponymous Shirley gives her husband chips and egg for his tea on a Thursday, when it's meant to be steak and chips for tea on a Thursday, and chips and egg for tea on a *Tuesday*. Her husband, Joe, played by Hill, gets very agitated when not only is his tea late, but it's also the wrong meal. He ends up angrily shoving the food at her, and it spills into her lap.

Later in the film Shirley leaves Joe to forge a new life for herself in Greece, and we hear him accusing her of making him a laughing stock. The understated realities in this film are well observed and capture some of the nuances of coercive control.

I thought of that chips and egg scene when I met Pete: his personal insight into his own situation was enlightening for me. Just as the jealousy and loyalty codes open the door to instilling and maintaining control, routine and ritual function not only as methods of control, but as an early-warning system to perpetrators that their control is being challenged. Pete and I met to talk about his life: given his situation, this was a big step for Pete. He knew that he was unhappy and he knew that his marriage was not good; he also knew that he wanted to leave his wife.

I think Pete knew what was wrong, but he did not trust himself; it was as if he needed some validation. He needed someone else to say: 'This is not right.'

We sat next to each other in a coffee shop and nobody would have guessed what we were talking about. Pete is a professional man who has responsibilities in his place of work; he

111

does not appear to be subservient or lacking in confidence in any way. Many women in this position who sit and talk with me disclose how frightened they are. But Pete doesn't say this; he doesn't tell me he is frightened.

'So what prompted you to want to talk to me?' I ask.

He smiles and looks down for a couple of seconds, then looks me straight in the eyes. 'I'm not allowed to choose what I eat; it's so tightly controlled,' he says. 'I'm not even allowed to say how much I want. She cooks when she gets in. I don't always know when that will be, but I have to wait.'

Pete stops talking for a minute, just thinking, organising his experience into something that makes sense, maybe for me, but probably, and more importantly, for him.

One thing I know is that this is not about eating, and it isn't just about Pete's wife – who he has been married to for twenty years – controlling his diet. It is much bigger than that.

'I brought home some pre-packaged stuffed mushrooms one day,' he continues. 'I'd been told they were really nice and I wanted to try them. She just took them out of my hand and put them in the freezer, saying they were unhealthy. When I went to get them out of the freezer the next day, they were gone. In the bin, probably.'

'Why were you looking for them?' I ask.

He looks at me and smiles. 'You're right to ask,' he says. 'I couldn't have cooked them, and I knew they'd be gone. It was like confirmation of what I had become. I wouldn't have dared cook them anyway.'

'Why?' I ask.

'Because it would have been a statement; it would have been a defiance. After all these years going along with the rules, to cook the mushrooms now would have been like declaring war.

I didn't honestly think I would win, so best not to start something I couldn't predict or handle the ending of.'

'So how often are you avoiding the start of war?'

'Well, it's strange, but as I stood there with the freezer door open,' he says, 'my legs were getting really cold, and I looked around the kitchen and, not for the first time, I realised that I was a trespasser: this wasn't my home, my life. I had no right to open the freezer and take food – I just had permission. But I knew I didn't have permission to eat those mushrooms. It hadn't been said, but we both knew that I knew. The coldness on my legs, it was giving me confidence. Then I started to get scared the food in the freezer would defrost and she would go crazy. So I shut the door.'

Pete turns his eyes from me and puts his head down.

'Where was she when you did that?' I ask.

'She was at work,' he says, making eye contact again.

'So do you often do what you're not supposed to when she's not there, when it's just you?'

'Not really. I'm really boring,' he replies. 'I do much the same thing every day. Hmmm . . . I drive to work at six o'clock, I get home at six thirty in the evening. It's funny thinking about how boring I am. I always thought I was so rebellious when I was young. I've been wearing the same cologne for twenty years! How boring is that?'

'Well, I guess you like it,' I say. 'Try a different one, maybe?'

I say this purposefully so that Pete will have to think about what is stopping him changing his cologne.

Pete thinks for a while. 'No,' he says. 'I'd need a reason. If I changed it, and I have thought about it, she would want to know why. She'd think I was having an affair or something.

I have to keep everything exactly the same. Any changes and she picks up on it. I have to be very careful. One night I was watching TV, but it was something I hadn't seen before. When she came in she wanted to know why I was watching it; it just turned into an argument because she didn't believe my reason. But I didn't have a reason – I was just watching it. I was making it up as I went along, and then it went on to other stuff and it kind of got to her accusing me of something.'

'So you're doing things the same because changes start trouble?' I say.

'The things in the house,' he continues, 'they have to be just so. I can't change anything. The cupboards are organised in a certain way, the towels must face a certain way, I mustn't alter anything. It's like I am a guest in the house; it's not my home, it's not my rules and it's always on a knife-edge. It's not like it's a thing about being tidy, she's not tidy, but she has things almost like it's a trap. I long for an escape, if I'm honest.'

'Have you ever thought about leaving?' I ask.

'All the time,' says Pete. 'But she would fight me, and she's so nasty. She would make my life hell. I can't buy a bottle of whisky by myself – how am I going to get the guts to leave?'

He picks up his coffee and thinks about taking a sip, but then puts it down and says with some vigour: 'I did bring it up about three years ago. First she just broke down sobbing and begging, then she was vicious and said some awful things. Then she told me about this really serious illness she was getting checked out at the doctor's; she said me leaving would kill her.'

'What happened after that?' I ask.

'I realised then that leaving was out of the question. Whatever I planned I knew she would destroy it. The day after that conversation she had a couple of her friends round, and they were talking about me, and she was crying. I knew I was being accused of having affairs and all sorts. They all sat there hating me.'

'What frightens you about leaving the most? Do you think she would hurt you physically?'

Pete thinks for a moment before speaking. 'I never really thought about that. I just think, more than attacking me physically, you know, that she would destroy me. Really destroy me from every direction. If she did assault me – and she does hit me when she gets angry – and I defended myself, I just know she would say I attacked her. That scares me; I don't want a record. I feel weak for being frightened of her, because I can't even tell you how, but I know she would destroy me. I have to be ready for that; I have to have a plan. I just never seem to have everything I need.'

Similar to Pete, Henri was less frightened of serious violence from Simone, but he was anxious about the chaos she created. Sometimes Simone had frightened Henri, and the pushing and shoving felt like it might get out of hand. However, he had been more concerned he might have to use violence himself, in self-defence, and how that would look; sometimes she would threaten to harm herself and Henri would worry about her mental health and seek help for her, but not for himself.

Pete's wife seemed to be controlling every aspect of his life. It is not as simple as a set of rules to follow, where there is freedom as long as the rules are not broken – a bit like the parent–child relationship. It is very different from that. It is a more generalised subjugation: the jealousy and the expectation of devout loyalty directing every interaction and infusing meaning into every choice.

The monitoring of Pete's behaviour was made easy because he had been so compliant. There were booby traps everywhere, designed to make any failure to comply highly visible. Any change in behaviour or expression of choice would be interpreted as disloyalty or challenge, and, more importantly, an alarm that control was weakening.

Pete's wife was very similar to Simone in that she micromanaged her husband's life by making him standardise his own behaviour and routines, reducing his world to something she could dominate and regulate. Once this kind of micro-regulation is achieved, even the tiniest change becomes highly visible and can be used to pre-empt and crush any more significant challenges. This delicate balance means that even cooking a couple of mushrooms can be interpreted as a sign of the ultimate defiance and plotting, and in many ways it can become that. Planning to leave would be a very difficult thing to do, underpinned with real fear of the consequences.

*

People who are controlling, resentful or vindictive may present more risk than those who take rejection or challenge more in their stride. We all know people who hang on to grudges and act on them. It may be a sign that they have control issues and a more fragile sense of self. People, male or female, who insist that 'no one talks to me like that' or who demand respect as a right, may be less able to deal with rejection or challenge.

Separation is known to be a key trigger for pushing controlling people to a tipping point, where the response can be extreme. Controlling people always have the potential for separation in their minds; it is their biggest fear and paranoia.

Simone's behaviour shows that the separation does not have to be real: it can be imagined and believed. It was subtle changes in Henri's behaviour and a perceived act of defiance and disloyalty that may have prompted the escalation in control. He did not comply with a demand to get into a battle, and that failure to comply was a sign to Simone of disloyalty and that her will was being challenged, that her control was weakening.

Constant accusations of infidelity or disloyalty are a warning marker that a person may be preoccupied with such thoughts, knowing they could not deal with the possibility. But it would be wrong to feel that this is a weakness in them that can be healed through showing enough love to 'cure' them of their fears. Most controlling people are not broken by separation in the way we might think; they are more often outraged by it. It is not necessarily the loss of the individual they are guarding against, but the loss of the relationship. Some controlling people have multiple relationships running simultaneously – having affairs outside a marriage, for example – but they will be as controlling of every partner.

Pete feels trapped by the potential outrage and anger he knows his leaving will provoke. So he stays, waiting for an opportunity, keeping things calm and even. This perfectly mirrors the lives of Donna and Bonnie; it is a part of coercive control we find difficult to understand.

Control is devious and deceptive, and these things are often invisible. People can see violence, they can hear threats, they can see tears and hear pleas, but they cannot see the control – not unless they believe it is there. Gavin de Becker says clearly that we need to believe before we can see. When we cannot see any violence and we cannot hear any threats, when all that is left is the control, it is the perfect undetectable storm.

Adults make choices, and victims are no exception. Pete's choice to stay with his wife was based on a cost–benefit analysis. Bonnie made a similar decision weighing up the consequences of leaving Karl. When we look at some of the choices victims make, and they do not look like the choices we think we would make, or we misinterpret what is going on, we can actually, inadvertently, strengthen the controlling person's hand.

The web of control

Control is not simple, and rarely one-dimensional. Multiple types of control interweave to form what can feel like an inescapable web.

For example, financial abuse adds another layer that not only restricts what someone can do but creates another hurdle to be conquered if the person is to leave. Maybe they do not have a bank account; maybe they have no access to money at all. Maybe their partner manages all the bills. It might be that the victim is the earner and the controlling person is dependent on them. This is just as powerful in terms of trying to leave. It could be very difficult to fund two homes, or to make someone homeless. I have seen cases where controlling people have given up work deliberately, then using their time to monitor and surveille their partner. The way someone spends their money may be strictly monitored, with questions asked and judgements made, even if their access to money is not restricted. There are many ways money and resources can be managed so that control is maintained. Benefits might be blocked or a person's credit record ruined. If a victim is to set up a new home with children, obtaining accommodation with a poor credit history or lack of deposit will be almost impossible.

A web of control can also include the knowing or unknowing collusion of others. In the case of Jasmine, her marriage was arranged, and she went to live with her in-laws. She knew no one and had no friends or contacts in the area. The next eighteen years were awful for her. She became something akin to a slave, performing all the menial domestic chores in the home, and was controlled by the entire extended family. Her freedom was limited through monitoring by her parents-in-law, her husband, the extended family and, as time went on, her own children. Jasmine felt trapped with no way out; she did not think leaving was a possibility. She had no support and nowhere to go, and she knew her husband and his parents would just bring her back if she did manage to leave. Jasmine eventually took her own life, and her suicide letter revealed her distress and isolation.

This type of community monitoring can be seen in many types of family groups and communities, but is especially well illustrated when thinking about so-called honour-based violence (HBV). The British charity Karma Nirvana was set up to help people in just this sort of situation. I was speaking at an event in Birmingham where they were raising awareness of the problems associated with HBV, which can also sometimes end with homicide. The parallels between the processes and motivations of some forms of HBV and the eight stages of the Homicide Timeline are so very similar, and this was discussed at the event. The motivation to manipulate or force someone to comply is the same, and it is threats to that control and the victim's attempts to challenge it that can end in an HBV death. In Jasmine's case, she took her own life, seeing escape as impossible.

Escape is also made more difficult when there are threats to those who matter to the victim. Even pets can be employed as a threat: some controlling people will threaten to euthanise a pet, or may hurt it or withdraw its food. If a pet has been a trusted companion in an isolated life, this may be a terrible fear. More common is the use of children to control and threaten.

Amita was a young woman who had been kept pregnant for the whole of her relationship with Muhammad. He would force sex on her and she was not allowed to use contraception. Amita was terrified of defying Muhammad and was desperate to leave him. He had broken all her fingers at various points, and rape was a regular occurrence. They had five children under ten years old and Muhammad had given up work to make sure he could keep an eye on Amita. He was at home all the time. When he did leave the house, she told me, he would always take at least one of the children with him. 'He knows I won't go, not without my children,' she said. 'So he keeps one of them with him. I won't go: I wouldn't leave them with him, I couldn't do it. They're my children. So I'm stuck.'

Amita had a friend; I spoke to both of them together. The friend had been nodding her head and agreeing with everything that Amita had been telling me. 'I don't know what I'd do without Bushra,' said Amita, nodding towards the friend. 'She keeps me sane.'

Bushra smiled and said: 'I hate him, I hate him with a passion, but if I ever let him know that, I'd be banned. I'd never get in the house again, and then she'd be on her own. I never say a word. I always smile and I'm really friendly. I hate it, but I've got no choice. What can we do?'

Here, Bushra is in the web of manipulation. She does not challenge Muhammad. In fact, no one does. He behaves as he does with impunity. The longer this goes on, the more power he has. Bushra is a lifeline, but she has to be complicit in the control to achieve that. A terrible dilemma for her.

'I'm terrified that the courts might give the children to him because no one knows,' says Amita. 'They all think everything's okay. If I ever told anyone – well, I mean, if he found out, he'd kill me, literally.'

I remember reading a story when I was researching one of my books, where a woman said that her husband used to threaten to physically punish their children, but gave her the choice. He said that either he would do it, or she could. The woman ended up hitting the children, knowing it would be a softer assault than if he did it. Of course, any interviews with the children would reveal to social services that it was Mummy who hit them. I have been told about women giving their children sedatives so they do not wake up in the night and cry and make a controlling person angry. Some children start to abuse a victim at the encouragement of a controlling person. All these things are traumatic for children. We tend to think that children 'witness abuse', but they do not merely witness: they are experiencing it; they are abused.

*

Family courts can actually be complicit in this control. There is a campaign spreading internationally that is highlighting this problem. The Court Said is a non-profit organisation challenging the family court system and its discriminatory practices. There is a flow of examples of outrageous comments and decisions made by judges and lawyers in the family court system and this campaign is having real influence in highlighting the need for change in the family courts.

Putting a victim in a courtroom with someone who has control over them, and who frightens them, will never get to the truth. The adversarial system makes an assumption that everyone's up for a fight and no one is scared. This is rarely the case. In its arrogance, the system even assumes that it has control over both parties and that its word is final. The flaws in this are made clear daily as perpetrators openly breach orders and conditions imposed by courts. It is a problem that, too often, courts do not take these breaches seriously. Coercive control is all about winning; it is a complicated and sinister game where the rules of society and the legal system stack the odds against the victim and leave them unprotected, and sometimes dead.

But the campaigns are mounting, and these are spreading globally. The family court system is under huge pressure to reform and become more informed and more open. The system would benefit from recognising control tactics that can paralyse victims or make them appear 'hysterical' while the perpetrator looks calm and reasonable.

I participated in a *Panorama* documentary about domestic violence and police body-worn cameras. A police camera had captured the moment two officers answered a 999 call put in secretly by a woman who had been severely beaten. Her husband, who had beaten her, did not know she had called the police.

The violence was shocking, and this is what the video captured. But more astonishing for me was to listen to the description of the campaign of control told by the victim. She mentioned code words used by her abuser to let her know how to behave. These code words and other signs would not be recognised or detected by others, and may have given the impression that the abuser was not controlling his victim. Code words and special 'looks' are regularly used in court proceedings, both civil and criminal, to undermine the testimony of victims. This victim also told of the way violence was used. Her husband knew that she was ashamed of the abuse and that she would not go out if she had visible injuries. She worked as a volunteer in a charity shop, but her husband did not like her going there. On the day before she was to return to work after a period of illness, he beat her in a planned and rational attack, just so she would be too ashamed to go to her job. His violence was not spontaneous, and he was not a martyr to his uncontrollable temper. This and the control tactics were planned, rational and sadistic.

Sexual abuse

Sexual abuse is nearly always present in coercive control in some way. It is a particularly nasty but effective way in which people, especially women, can be subjugated. It can also be a particularly nasty but effective defence to homicide.

It is not unusual for sexual force to be described by perpetrators as 'playful' or consensual. Then frightening or nasty sexual assaults can be described afterwards as 'only messing about', or the victim's fault, and victims can be accused of 'overreacting', or not being open enough in their own sexual behaviour. The word 'vanilla' is used as an insult, just as words like 'frigid' are still used, where victims are made to feel inadequate. These words can be used to manipulate women and girls into consenting to sexual acts that frighten, hurt, harm or distress them. There has been a rise in 'sex game gone wrong' defences in court, otherwise referred to as the '*Fifty Shades* defence'.

The surge in this particular defence is quite shocking, and the cruelty in the alleged sexual practices quite disturbing. The death of twenty-six-year-old Natalie Connolly in 2016 attracted a lot of attention for the severity of the injuries she suffered that led to her death, including a fractured eye socket, said by her partner to be inflicted in a sex game. He was convicted of manslaughter and sentenced to three years and eight months. The death of Grace Millane, a British tourist who died in New Zealand in 2018, also received a lot of attention after it was claimed by her killer that she died during consensual strangulation. He was convicted of murder and sentenced to seventeen years.

The UK-based group We Can't Consent to This started a campaign after looking at the frequency with which it is claimed that victims were killed during allegedly consensual dangerous sexual gameplay. Most often the defence rests on claims that women enjoy being strangled during sex, often to unconsciousness. The first time I saw this defence being given wide coverage was in the trial of Graham Coutts for the murder of music teacher Jane Longhurst. Her killer, who was not an intimate partner, claimed she liked being strangled and that her death was accidental. He also had a large repository of strangulation pornography; she did not. The pathologist said that Coutts would have been aware of a medical emergency for some three minutes before Jane died. The 'rough sex' defence has now been weakened in the UK through the upcoming Domestic Abuse Bill. It was announced in June 2020 that no one would be able to use the argument that there was consent where serious injury or death occurred during sex, and so reduce charges or avoid an investigation.

Strangulation is the most common life-threatening abusive practice used in both a sexual and a non-sexual context in domestic abuse. There is a very strong link between strangulation assaults and homicide. Any practice that restricts breathing or makes someone feel their life is at risk is a very powerful method of control and gives an insight into what the controlling person might be willing to do. I am not saying that the link is there because sometimes the strangulation accidentally kills someone, far from it; the link is there because people who use strangulation as a tactic of control are more likely to kill their partner deliberately.

In some states in America, strangulation is considered a stand-alone assault, and in most states it must be charged as a felony (indictable offence) and not a misdemeanour (summary offence). This is because of its links to homicide. It has also been found that it is linked to future stroke and PTSD in all age groups.

The blanket assumption should never be that anyone suffering control would consent to potentially fatal practices, or that a fetish for strangulation is widespread in women. There are reports that women, and especially young women, are increasingly being pressured into strangulation by their partners. Most report they are frightened by it and find it painful, not arousing. The practice also has dangerous links to long-term illness, even in young women. The practice of auto-erotic asphyxiation (restricting your own breathing for sexual arousal) has long been associated with men. There is an obvious difference between strangling someone else for sexual arousal and strangling yourself. People who enjoy watching others struggle for breath are being aroused by a different stimulant from those who enjoy starving themselves of oxygen. There has been a rise in controlling men claiming that their partners ask to be strangled, but the research is not there to support the idea that strangulation is a widespread female fetish. A survey conducted by Stand Up To Domestic Abuse (SUTDA) and myself asking about non-fatal strangulation found that in over 90 per cent of cases, there was no consent, and it was in fact being used as means to terrify and hurt. The assumption – especially where there is evidence of coercive control, stalking or domestic abuse – should be that women or men do not ask their abuser to strangle them, not that they do.

Indeed, where there has been documented or witnessed domestic violence and coercive control, we should never assume the victim just made hard-to-understand decisions.

The rise of so-called 'revenge porn' to maintain control is another form of sex-based abuse. There is a rise in – especially, but not always – partners manipulating or pressurising their female or male partners to share intimate films or photos. Photographs may be freely given by victims but later used against them to maintain control, punish, frighten or trap them; photos and films may be taken without their consent or even their knowledge. These images may then be used if the relationship ends or if there is some breakdown in control. Either way there has also been a rise in the prosecution and reporting of this offence – though many offences are never reported – and there is greater support and advice for people threatened in this way, such as support through the Revenge Porn Helpline.

This is why the conversations have to change: we should be more sceptical of such claims and accept that a history of coercive control means that free choice and consent in that relationship may be entirely absent – and that abuse, manipulation and sometimes cruelty will be present.

*

Stage three, then, is all about making sure a partner is compliant and trapped within the relationship. All victims are different and will be controlled in different ways.

Victims with learning or physical disabilities, for instance, face some different challenges, as do older victims; male and female victims face different challenges, as do young people and people from the LGBT+ communities. Control is not practised in one particular way: the victims and their controlling partners are diverse and distinct. What we can recognise are patterns where different methods are used to achieve the same aim – like the jealousy code, the loyalty code, and routines and rituals. We should not therefore just expect to see bruises and broken bones; if we do that, we are only focusing on the Karls, and completely missing the Vincents and the Simones, who are potentially equally dangerous.

Stage three can last a lifetime. If there are no challenges to the control, or the challenges are effectively overcome and defeated, then both partners may stay in the relationship until they die. I have looked at cases where stage three lasted three weeks, or as long as fifty-four years. The length of stage three rather depends on the emergence of stage four, and what happens as a result.

4

Stage Four: Trigger

When Tom Jones sang about the murder of Delilah, we all sang along. We celebrated the crime of passion where a man kills *his* woman because she cheated on him in a resounding and infectious chorus; the words tell of possession of the woman, and her murder as revenge for infidelity. The entire 'crime of passion' narrative is there in those few words.

There is even a word – cuckold – that describes a man whose wife is sexually deceiving him, a man who has been emasculated by the deception. 'Delilah' is the anthem of the emasculated cuckold. But digging down into those two words and the fact they even exist reveals the importance of possession, control and power to 'masculinity'. (Note that 'masculinity' is not the same as 'men': 'masculinity' is a behavioural model that we impose on men and is adopted by some women. There are different ways of performing 'masculinity', but there is definitely a dominant model that is favoured and given more status.) There are few powerful insults to throw at men, and it is interesting that 'emasculated cuckold', which is among the most powerful, swivels on losing control of a possession or status.

Much as this song and the crime-of-passion fairy tale it celebrates may feel like common sense, Delilah and her man are just characters, and no more realistic than Cinderella and

Prince Charming. They are idealised versions of the main players in a performance of intimate partner homicide. He is the emasculated cuckold pushed to claw back his status; she, unfaithful, is the uncaring, laughing assassin of his masculinity. They are powerfully symbolic.

However, in reality, the trigger to homicide is rarely a happened-upon infidelity.

Stage four is the trigger stage: it is a happening that means something has changed or is changing for the controlling person. It means that they may be losing something they want and feel entitled to. For some, anything they want is something they are entitled to, but for some, society sets the rules for what they feel entitled to. An entitlement is like a right – and you can legitimately fight for your rights. To lose your rights, or give them up without a fight, can mean a loss of status.

Status measured by seniority is very important to some people – it is fundamental to everything they do. They may seek to increase it, they may have an inflated sense of it, they may measure what they think they deserve by the rights their perceived status implies. These are more than basic human rights; these may be cultural, religious, historical or other perceived rights.

Vincent felt he knew his place in the world and his status, and he felt Donna was taking away those meagre entitlements when she said she wanted to separate.

Control or possession of a partner might well be perceived as a right, but control is also a measure of how intact that right is. Once control of the partner diminishes, once things start to change, the whole house of cards might be about to topple.

Separation

Although separation is the most common trigger by far, any change can be associated with potential separation and loss of control of the relationship. For example, the threat of financial ruin, bankruptcy, retirement, redundancy or illness. Controlling people rarely like it when change is pushed upon them. They prefer the status quo.

A victim who has developing dementia, for example, may be unable to respond to control in the same way they used to: their partner may not be willing to look after their needs, and they may also resent the interference of health professionals, who will inevitably start to influence decisions. They may resent not being the centre of their partner's attention. It should never be assumed that the killing of partners who are ill is a 'mercy' killing, not if there has been a history of coercive control. If the controlling person becomes ill, they may lose their ability to exert control and this too can be intolerable to them.

The tipping point or the trigger is not simply jealousy. Women rarely kill their partners when they leave them. They are more likely to kill in self-defence or in fear of harm to themselves or their children, and they are more likely to kill themselves than their partner. Is this because women do not get jealous? We know that is not true, but we also know that the cultural script is that women are expected to tolerate infidelity and affairs, and they are expected to tolerate being controlled and taking a less active position more generally. There is also less pressure on women to maintain the kind of status of men.

Some women, like Simone, will behave very similarly to men where their status, control and sense of self are threatened. It is a fact that men resort to murder more often than women, and there are complex reasons for that, including the influences of biology, psychology and culture. I do think a common thread is that women do not generally get taught that they have ownership of men – quite the opposite: they are more often taught that they are owned.

Vincent, for example, knew Donna was planning to leave him. She had told him that. Vincent probably felt a number of things. He was concerned that life as he knew it would change too much; he felt that Donna had no right to leave him; he felt he was suffering yet another injustice in his life; he may have felt humiliated.

Karl was very angry with Bonnie when she would not withdraw the complaint of assault she had made against him. He could not stop the prosecution and he could not stop her leaving his sphere of control; he was frustrated. By killing her, he punished her and retrieved some status. He also effectively stopped her, as he saw it, from wielding any more power over him, and he stopped the prosecution.

Simone was outraged that Henri did not show solidarity when she felt she was suffering an injustice at the hands of his business colleagues. She felt he should have stood by her and recognise the injustice she was suffering. She was also paranoid that this was a sign he was going to leave her and that was something she could not tolerate.

Another layer to the way controlling people respond to triggers was revealed to me by chance when I was interviewing another killer, named Devin, who was serving a life sentence for killing his girlfriend. There are moments in life that are game changers. They are flashes that have the power to influence or change the way you think about something. For me, one of those moments happened when I was chatting to Devin in a tiny meeting room in a category-A prison. He revealed to me, quite inadvertently, how he understood what was and was not acceptable in terms of violence against a partner, and how that links with a trigger.

Devin

Devin was already sitting in the meeting room when I arrived. It was the smallest room, too small, and I felt uncomfortably close to the young man who was sitting opposite me, backed against a wall. He greeted me with a smile and was polite and friendly. Only in his twenties, he had a vulnerability about him that did not match the horrific record of his violence. As we reflected on his life, I sensed that vulnerability was probably quite real. Violence and neglect had dislocated his life and developed into a determined and relentless spectre at his shoulder, at first uninvited, and then embraced.

Devin's accent meant I had to listen carefully; he had a lilting Scottish drawl which he peppered with colloquialisms. He leaned back in his chair, pushing it onto two legs in a very casual and macho way, taking all the space he could; he seemed to want to give me the impression that he was a big, powerful man, confident and unconcerned. I felt he was almost desperate to give this impression. In contrast to Vincent, Devin did not want to look like a victim, but he did want me to know about events in his life that told of victimisation.

'My dad was a bastard,' he said. 'He was in charge. But I wasn't having any of it. When my mum went, it was worse.

I would've wanted to go with her, but I couldn't – he wasn't having it.'

Devin's father was a brutal man. It is almost unnecessary to expand on that statement. Brutal people create a world of pain around them and that pain is carried forward. For Devin, that pain was the architect of his relationship with the world, and it was visited on his wife and children. That the chain reaction ended with his wife's death and his own incarceration is unlikely. His children, now without mother or father, and victims of his brutality, as he was of his father's, are in pain, and so it goes on. The destructive legacy of abusive people is a social fact.

For his part, Devin was determined that he would be the one making the choices, he would be the abuser, not the victim. He did that classic thing: he split the world into winners and losers. He may have felt more like a loser inside, but he wanted the world to see a winner. 'I had a knife fight with my father. I was only about thirteen or fourteen,' he told me. 'It got really bad, but I'd had enough and he threw me out. I didn't have nowhere to go, and I slept most nights on the streets in Glasgow or maybe at a mate's place.'

Devin was smiling as he said this, as though he was proud of his use of the knife, like it was giving him status. Even so, I did not feel that he was simply bragging; it felt more like he was determined that I did not see him as weak. Everything he did, from the way he sat in his chair, to the way he told his stories, was designed to display how 'hard' Devin was. I believe he was a man used to violence and happy to use it. I also think that he lived a life operating at the edges. But I do not believe that he *felt* 'hard'. Not in that prison. It was clearly important to him, however, that I believed it.

I do not tell you these things to try and elicit sympathy for Devin, but to try and show that the control he felt he needed may have been rooted in insecurity and a fear of victimisation or abandonment. I am not arguing that all control issues come from insecurity, but most control issues come from *somewhere*.

A powerful and insidious source that we often dismiss is socialisation. Boys are in many ways socialised to believe and expect that they are entitled to be in control of their families: that it is the way of things, a biological imperative. This sets both an expectation and a pressure. Men may defend that absolute right, feeling entirely justified, by enforcing their control in any way they can. To lose that control, or to have it usurped, can feel like humiliation, weakness and failure. I was fascinated to read that most displays of power, most fights over inconsequential and trivial things between men, most shows of anger, are for the benefit of other men, not women. There is a huge pressure to maintain status.

Certainly all these things seemed to converge in Devin's life, and his wife was the focus for all potential attacks on his self-esteem and his masculine rights. The whole thing played out as domestic violence and coercive control.

Devin was so terrified that his wife might leave him that he would often lock her in at night, ensuring she could not make a run for it when he was sleeping. Violence was a language he knew well, and he used it with paralysing effect. Not only did he physically force his will on her, he used every means available to him to subjugate her. One of the most powerful, even more powerful than the physical violence, was the use of forced pregnancy. Devin made sure she was constantly pregnant – and with every child she was more tightly tied to him.

Pregnancy is a time when coercive control and domestic abuse can become more visible. Some say that this is when it starts, but it is equally possible that pregnancy is a tipping point or a trigger that provokes an escalation in controlling behaviours that makes them more visible. When a woman becomes pregnant her priorities may change, and medical professionals and family may become more influential and interested. This can be a real pressure for a controlling person, and so their control tactics escalate and what was always there becomes more visible and severe.

In contrast, people like Devin, who see pregnancy and child-rearing as a method to trap and control their partners, will keep them pregnant. Not only are pregnant women physically vulnerable, they are more financially and emotionally dependent. Devin's girlfriend was only twenty-four when she died; she had four children. She was desperate to leave Devin: she could not take any more pregnancies; she could not take any more of his control and violence. She was a very young woman with a lot of responsibilities, and a lot of fear and anxiety in her life.

Devin had a record with the police for violence against her. There were many times when she and others had called the police because of this behaviour. I asked him about this.

'I was never violent to her,' he said to me.

'But the police tell me that they were called many times to your house because you were hitting her.'

'It wasn't domestic violence,' he answered. 'We planned it together. If they thought she was a victim, like if I was hitting her, they would have to rehouse her and we needed a new flat. It was never domestic violence. That's just not true – we did it together.'

'Are you saying,' I asked him, 'that you were never violent to her?'

'Never,' he replied. 'We planned it, I'm telling you. I had to get arrested to make it look true.' He was looking at me intently; he really wanted me to believe this.

'Are you saying that every accusation she made against you was part of a plan to upgrade your housing or receive benefits?'

'That's right. It was never domestic violence. Never. We planned it together, you know.'

Every accusation or conviction for violence was explained to me as something they both made up to get benefits, or to secure housing, or some other ruse. He did not admit or acknowledge that he had beaten, controlled and terrorised her.

We know that Devin had, in fact, terrorised her, because she confided in social workers and midwives, and anyone who would listen, just how awful life was with him. It was also witnessed by others. She was determined to get away from him and determined not to have any more children with him.

Devin suddenly rolled up the sleeve on his sweatshirt to reveal a large tattoo, which looked quite raw and new. He said he had had it done in the prison. He did not tell me exactly why he was showing me. It was certainly a diversion from the conversation, and Devin wanted to talk about it. He was definitely not comfortable talking about domestic violence.

He further deflected the conversation and started to tell me lots of stories of his cunning and ingenuity surviving on the streets of Glasgow. Some of the stories were patently not true, but he seemed to want me to know he had status within his prison peer group, that he could hold his own and was respected by the other men. He revealed that status was important to him; it was all he wanted to talk about. Just as being a victim was all Vincent talked about, and petty disputes all Simone talked about, Devin revealed much about himself.

And then, very quietly, there was the game-changing moment...

Crossing the line

'There's a guy in here,' Devin continued. 'Nasty bastard. If I get my hands on him, I'm going to kill him. He beat his wife. He was always beating her; there was no need for that, you know. Then he beat her to death. That guy, he crossed a line.'

I was astounded at this comment. He was saying, with no sense of irony, that this man who had beaten and kicked his wife to death, had 'crossed a line'. I had to wonder what exactly that line was, given that Devin had stabbed his own girlfriend to death in public in front of many witnesses. He used a knife he had purchased just for the task. But in his head he had not crossed whatever line it was he was referring to.

That comment dominated my thoughts for weeks and months afterwards. If Devin thought he had not crossed this unwritten line, then the line exists. Somewhere in his world that line had been drawn by someone, a line that set the parameters for the abuser's code of conduct. It seems that not crossing this line helped him feel justified in what he did, and why he did it. He was *morally superior* to the other man. I thought about some of the things Devin had said to me from the perspective that there was a line and that he considered – or wanted others to consider – that he had not crossed it.

First, Devin would not admit to domestic violence. He claimed that he and his girlfriend had colluded to make it look as if he was an abuser. He was not distancing himself from using violence, but he drew the line at people thinking he beat or terrorised his girlfriend. So at some level Devin seemed to share, or at least be aware of, the ethical parameters of society. He knew what he was doing was wrong.

Second, he separated the use of general violence from the use of homicidal violence. Devin had killed for a reason; he felt he was justified, and that was okay. Murder was an action that had enough masculine cachet for him to admit to it. But beating a woman – that was for cowards. However, he did beat his girlfriend. Regularly. He was not just trying to minimise the judicial response to his violence, it was wider than that. The respect of his peers was important to him. He associated respect with power and safety. At some level he thought his peers would not respect domestic violence, but would respect domestic homicide. He was not a wife-beater – he was a wife-killer.

I had to let that sink in to make sense of what I had heard. I found that small comment was now more frightening than I had at first considered it to be. Devin felt justified when he stabbed his girlfriend to death. He felt he would have the support and respect of his peers, of the court, of society. Similar, in a way, to Vincent, who also thought he would find solidarity and have the support of the courts and people who knew him.

Devin, like Vincent, Karl and Simone, never mentioned his deceased partner by name for the entirety of our meeting. He never mentioned any of the suffering she endured in her short life. He never expressed any remorse – though I suspect there was shame in the subtext, in the lies about the abuse. But the shame in killing her appeared to be non-existent. The abuse, in whatever form, was to keep control. The homicidal violence was to express defensible outrage and mete out the ultimate control.

*

There is a theory put forward by criminologists Gresham Sykes and David Matza that says that criminals share the same moral and ethical codes as the rest of society and that criminals are able to excuse and justify what they do when they violate the norms of society. Sykes and Matza call these excuses *techniques of neutralisation*. These techniques which, broadly speaking, provide justifications for wrongdoing, allow people to continue their criminal activities with minimal damage to their sense of self and identity, and mitigate any criticism. This means that they remove responsibility by denying they have hurt anyone, or they claim they were more victimised than their victims. They compare themselves favourably to the people who might accuse them of wrongdoing and align themselves with a code of conduct they share with their peers.

Through my conversations with Devin, Simone, Vincent and Karl, I learned they all did this. They all, to some extent, blamed their past for their present selves, which takes some responsibility away; they all blamed the victim for provoking them, which also makes the victim take responsibility from them.

This is one of the reasons I found Devin's conversation about crossing a line so significant. He was telling me that in *his world*, there is a line, a moral code. In *his world* there is an understanding that killing your girlfriend is okay if you have the right justification.

So what is Devin's world where this moral code exists? The world of killers? It cannot be that, because he was not part of that community before killing his girlfriend. Was it the world of street criminals? That is not true either, because men from all socio-economic groups kill their girlfriends and claim similar justifications. Was it the world of domestic abusers? More probably, but he denies being part of that world. Was it the world of men? This has more potential, because it is predominantly men who commit these murders; however, it is not only men who believe these justifications. Devin's world, then, may well be the world we *all* inhabit. The world where we routinely accept that wives and girlfriends are killed in so-called crimes of passion; where they, the deceased, contributed to their own murders; where murder can be justified. Devin lives in this world, along with Vincent, Karl, Simone and the rest of us.

The next stage, stage five, is all about what happens when a controlling person is faced with a trigger, and how they try to claw back control.

5

Stage Five: Escalation

I met Micha's family when I was a trustee for the charity Protection Against Stalking (PAS), of which I am now a patron. Micha had been murdered by her former partner.

I was working on a campaign with PAS's founder, Tricia Bernal, MPs Alex Chalk and Richard Graham, and the Suzy Lamplugh Trust to increase the maximum sentence for the most dangerous stalkers. There was a lot of interest in the campaign and I presented a report into the links between stalking and homicide at the House of Commons. We were successful, and legislation was passed, seeing the maximum sentence double from five to ten years for the most dangerous stalkers.

It was, in fact, a judge in the criminal court who suggested a campaign be started. This judge had felt extremely frustrated that he could only sentence a man who had been relentlessly stalking a woman and her family to five years in prison. He thought that a tougher sentence had been needed and he talked about this in his sentencing remarks. The victim in that case, who worked as a GP, started the campaign. She lived locally to me and I was able to spend some time with her and talk about the effect the stalking had had. The stalker was not a former partner; he was a patient. The stalking had lasted nearly a decade and the impact on her and her family had been life-changing. It is over now, but only through some drastic actions taken by the victim and the imprisonment of the stalker. The fact that the campaign managed to double the maximum sentence allowed shows that knowledge of these patterns has grown and is recognised in the justice system. Stalking is now taken more seriously.

Micha's family had been talking to me about her murder as part of the report I presented in the campaign. They had some very interesting things to tell me about Paulo, the man who murdered her, especially about the way he behaved after Micha ended the relationship. Paulo had tried to convince Micha to stay with him and change her mind about separating. He could be charming and thoughtful one minute, and in the next breath become angry and insulting. Then he would try crying, then begging, then the anger would come back, and then the threats to kill himself. He left flowers by her car, he called her to negotiate, he followed her, and he told her in a very threatening way that she would regret her decision. It was a rollercoaster of different tactics. Those tactics formed a pattern of stalking.

Micha's mother told me about something Paulo did after the separation that made her feel very uncomfortable, though it was not threatening as such. One evening he turned up at her home unannounced, saying he wanted to talk about Micha – not to her, about her. Although she thought it strange, and she felt a bit uneasy, she invited him in, not really knowing what else to do. She was astounded when Paulo spent the next hour delivering a pre-prepared PowerPoint presentation outlining all the reasons why Micha should not leave him and why her family should get behind him and bring Micha back to her senses.

From any perspective this is a very odd thing to do, and it gives us some insight into Paulo. He was presenting what he considered to be a perfectly reasonable and logical case for Micha's mother to become involved in his web of control. It does seem astonishing that he felt she would do that once she had seen his business case. This was not a request; he was not asking for her help; he was pointing out the arguments why she should be talking sense into her daughter. He made an assumption that Micha's mother would or could be persuaded, and that she would stand in solidarity with him. Paulo did not recognise how bizarre his behaviour was; he could only see how right and justified he was.

Although the means of a PowerPoint is rather unusual, it is not unusual for controlling people to try and co-opt others to help them regain control. I have seen this in many cases. Sometimes friends are used unwittingly; sometimes family are approached to try and intervene. This kind of networking can form a web of control that not only traps victims more tightly, but can validate the idea that the controlling partner is entitled to behave in such a way.

When change happens – for instance, a separation – it may be natural to resist that change, but people like Paulo or Vincent or Karl may act quite intensively on those feelings to try to restore the status quo. In this stage all manner of tactics may be used, and it is important to recognise these tactics for what they are. Begging and crying can be incredibly powerful, and threats and insults can be frightening. Threats of suicide are very common and are more dangerous than they might appear; they should always be considered worrying. If someone is contemplating their own death at this stage, they may have a very final view of the situation and this can be highly dangerous. I always advise that a suicide threat at this stage should be read as a threat to homicide.

Complexity runs through all these situations, and there is no one way that things will play out. How they unfold depends on complicated individual circumstances and personalities.

When we think about what Sada said in her diaries about Rohan proposing to her when she told him she was leaving, this was an escalation-stage strategy for him, and it worked. Vincent tried everything: begging, buying flowers, making threats to kill himself, and also making threats to harm Donna, but she did not relent. Donna was clear she wanted to leave. In cases where the separation actually happens, it is highly likely that stalking may begin. This is what happened to Micha.

Stalking

It comes as a shock to many that the most prevalent and dangerous category of stalker is an ex-partner. Flowers from a lover are very different from flowers from a stalker, and sometimes things can be complicated when the sender of the flowers is both.

Stalking is a complex pattern, and it has no strict legal definition. The UK definition, such as it is, gives a non-exhaustive list of possible behaviours; it also says that the victim must be alarmed or distressed by the patterns. This does cause a problem in some cases, because stalking is often clandestine. Sometimes a victim will not know they are being stalked, and this leaves a conundrum for the legal system. Stalking may be better defined through the intentions and motivations of the stalker than by the effect on the victim. A good example is the case of a dentist being stalked by a former patient of his in Wales in 2020. The dentist did not know he was being stalked, but the stalker had the intention, from the evidence found by police, to kill him. He had notes telling of his plans and what the judge described as a 'murder kit' in his car. He was reported to police by a member of the public who was alarmed to see him in his car with a balaclava on. It was not possible to charge him with the most serious stalking offence, the offence we had campaigned on and increased the sentencing on, because the victim had not known and was therefore not frightened. But the risk to the victim remained the same, whether or not they knew about it.

Stalking can include behaviours such as following, watching, tracking, monitoring, calling, texting and so on – all of which can be done physically or electronically; most often there will be a mix of both. Many controlling people will have been monitoring and tracking their partners during the relationship, not just after it ends. However, legislation in the UK also does not recognise stalking in an intact relationship, so although these tracking and monitoring behaviours are very common, it is not until after a relationship ends that they are legally recognised as stalking.

Victims might have their phones, social media and internet activity tracked; they might hand over their passwords to partners, often as part of the jealousy code; GPS tracking software is sometimes placed on victims' phones, in their cars, and even in children's school bags. Stalking is a means through which intelligence can be gathered, and control or fear can be exerted from a distance. It is also a method that can track whether there are any challenges to the relationship or the control. Stalking is always a concerning behaviour, and in all situations indicates that fixated and obsessive patterns are present. The UK College of Policing have a useful mnemonic – FOUR – used to identify stalking:

F – Fixated
O – Obsessive
U – Unwanted
R – Repeated

The earlier that stalking patterns are identified, the better; the earlier they are disrupted or challenged, the more chance they will stop. I have found that many victims, especially in the early stages, may second-guess their own instincts. Sometimes things just seem strange and cannot be explained, but there is usually a reason that someone feels concerned.

Instinct is not an esoteric and unfathomable feeling. Very often it is the cumulative knowledge built from previous experiences and learning, sometimes subconscious. If someone thinks something is wrong, it is often because something they have seen or experienced links to a former experience, or just makes them suspicious. It is good to listen to our instincts.

One morning I was walking my children to school when my instincts caused me to be more observant. I have three children, so the walk to school was always quite chaotic, and this morning was no different. The school is on a fairly busy but narrow road, and there were children and parents everywhere, all over the pavements, and spilling onto the road. I was not openly looking for anything unusual, but I have finely tuned antennae now for strange behaviours; I tend to spot them, no matter what the context.

Up ahead, facing towards me, I could see a man sitting in the driver's seat of a parked car. There were parents and children all around the car and no one was taking any notice of him. He was sitting perfectly still and straight and looking forward. This was what caught my attention. Why would someone sit straight and still in such a place with such chaos around him? I would expect him to be moving, or chatting on a phone, or searching through a bag, or making to get out of the car. He was doing none of these things. Could he be asleep? Maybe he was dead? Although all these things went through my head, I knew what this was before I reached the car. I knew because I had seen it before. I kept walking, now unable to hear the chatter of my children, focused on him. I wanted to be able to just walk past the car as all the other parents were doing. I did not want him to see I had spotted him, and I did not want to frighten any children. I noted down his registration number and, as I came alongside the car, I looked sideways through the car window, gathering all the detail I could for the police call I would make when my children were safely in school.

I was right. Through the window I could see he was masturbating. Quietly but brazenly. No one else had noticed; everyone was busily going about their business and he raised no suspicions. But my instinct told me his body language was all wrong for the context. The police arrested him at the scene. They also found illegal images on his computer, related to children.

People will often dissuade you from trusting your instincts, and I am not sure what the benefit is. I always trust mine. I get told fairly regularly that I see abuse and risk everywhere, that in some way I might over-predict and therefore my instincts cannot be trusted. However, I know my instincts are sound.

So many times I have heard stalking victims described as 'paranoid' or 'fanciful', and domestic abuse victims as exaggerating or being attention-seeking. And I have seen those same people proved wrong time and time again. It's far more dangerous to tell people to ignore their instincts than to support them in reasonably considering their safety.

Ruby

I met with Ruby because she was being stalked. She did not know what to do. She had no idea who was doing it, but as a woman living alone with two children, she felt very vulnerable.

Stalking is uniquely damaging to its victims. They are manipulated into a state of hyper-vigilance; they never know when the next contact will happen or what that contact may be. They can never relax, and this can have catastrophic effects on their mental and physical health.

'Tell me what first made you worried you were being stalked,' I say to Ruby as we sit and chat over coffee.

'I think it started not long after I moved into my new house. I started getting these silent phone calls. The house phone would ring and when I answered there was nothing, just silence. No heavy breathing or anything.' She laughs, but it is a nervous laugh. 'I ignored it. After all, it could have been so many things. I didn't want to make a drama out of it.'

'I'm guessing things have got worse?'

'Yes, they've got worse. He started talking. He says he's watching me; he says he knows where I am and what I'm doing. He said he knows what I am wearing, and then one time he told me what I was wearing and he was right. I was terrified.'

'Do you have any ideas who it might be?' I ask.

'No I don't, but I guess it must be someone who knows me, because he's got my number.'

In most cases of stalking the victim will know their stalker. The most likely person is a former intimate partner, but sometimes it may be a colleague or acquaintance, patient or student, or even a complete stranger. I wanted to know more about Ruby's life to try and get a feel for who this might be.

'How long have you been separated from your husband and living alone?' I say.

'I split with Connor about six or seven months ago; we're getting divorced.'

'How was the split?'

'It wasn't good,' she says. 'Connor and me, we'd come to the end – he was cheating and he wasn't great to live with. The usual, you know. He was frightening me.'

'How is it now?'

'I'm happy now. I don't have to talk to him much, just about the kids. I'm with someone new, and I've never been happier.' She leans down into her large leather handbag and pulls out a purse. 'Here, let me show you a picture.' Flipping open the purse, she shows me a photograph of a dark-haired, smiling man. 'This is Jake,' she says.

The picture has been professionally done, not just a selfie, and shows Ruby and Jake looking relaxed and happy.

In this short conversation she has given me quite a lot of information. There has been a difficult divorce, and now there's an ex who is not entirely off the scene. There is a new partner, and this must have been a fairly recent but intense relationship. Ruby is still in the middle of her divorce, but the new relationship is established enough to have arranged to have a professional photo shoot. I feel she is very distracted by the new man.

'How long have you been seeing Jake?' I ask.

'Not that long, really – about two or three months.'

'How did you meet?'

'We're colleagues; we've been working together for a long time.'

'Is it serious?'

'Yes, I think so. We're going to be together and the kids think he's great – they love him,' she says, smiling.

'Does he live far from you? I mean, is he local?'

'He lives just up from my new house, quite close. I was living about ten miles away, when I was with Connor, but this new house is really convenient for us.'

'That's good, then,' I say.

'I'm hoping we'll be living together soon. I'll probably feel safer then, but Jake's got to sort out his marriage. He's leaving his wife so I have to keep my head down for a bit.'

Another complication enters the conversation. Jake is married.

'Is he still living with his wife?'

'For the moment. The marriage is over, just like mine, really. He just has to choose his time, you know. I know how difficult it is – I've just done it myself.'

'How did you and Jake realise that you wanted to be together?' I ask her.

'It was just a kind of spark between us. We were both really unhappy. Connor was horrible and I needed to leave, and Jake's wife is really horrible to him, so I suppose we had something in common. We were both so unhappy. But we're really happy when we're together.'

Ruby's eyes are shining.

'When do you think he'll move in, then?'

'I don't know. I have to admit I thought he'd have done it by now. We've had a couple of rows over it. Sometimes I think he's just too scared to leave. But there's nothing to stop him now.'

'Does his wife know about you?'

'No, we've kept a really low profile. I didn't really want Connor to find out either, because he can be really difficult. He's quite jealous and it's just best until things are sorted that no one knows. I don't know what I would have done without Jake, though. These phone calls have been really freaking me out. Usually I can call Jake and he'll come round and check the garden, and the locks and everything. That makes me feel better.' Ruby smiles.

'Have you told the police?' I ask.

'No, I haven't. I felt a bit silly. It's just phone calls. I didn't know if they would take it seriously. But now I'm getting more worried and Jake can't always be there. I'm worrying that one of the kids might answer the phone. It's getting on top of me.'

'What does Jake say about the calls?'

'He says it's probably nothing to worry about. It happens all the time, doesn't it?'

'You need to tell the police and get a trace on the line,' I say.

'But do you think I'm in danger? Do I have to worry?'

'You're already worried,' I reply. 'That's enough reason to find out who this is.'

Ruby agrees she will call the police. I strongly advise her not to tell anyone that she is going to the police, no one at all, not Jake or Connor or any of her friends.

*

A few weeks later Ruby and I meet again. She does not look happy at all. She has dark circles under her eyes and she is smoking a cigarette.

'I guess you have some news,' I say.

'Yes,' she replies. 'I know who it is, and I wish I didn't.'

'Who was it?' I ask.

'It was Jake.'

'I was worried it might be,' I say. 'I think you had your concerns too, didn't you?'

'I was getting suspicious that he always seemed to be there after a call, but they never happened when he was around.'

'Have you spoken to him?'

'Oh yes, I was so angry. I had to calm down a bit, but I had to have it out with him. Do you know what he said? He said he was so worried about losing me and he loved me so much that he had to try and stop me leaving him. I had told him I was getting fed up waiting for him to make up his mind about his wife. He said he did it to make me frightened, so I'd need him more. He said he knew I'd call him if I got a silent call. He said he did it because he's just so frightened of losing me.'

There had been strong clues that Jake was controlling, and stalking is nearly always about control. The first for me was the speed with which the relationship started, but maybe more important was the fact that Jake wanted to get commitment and control over Ruby's life and home without him making a commitment. We reflect on that.

'Jake helped me to look for the new house, so that I could be away from my ex-husband; he promised to have a joint mortgage and live with me as soon as his divorce was finalised, but of course when the signing of the sale documents was due, he had not been able to get the money, as his wife was "performing" again and refusing to sign the divorce papers. Probably the luckiest escape that I had: the house was signed in my name only.'

She lights another cigarette.

'Looking back, all the warnings were there. I remember saying I couldn't see him one night and that he should go to the pub with his mates. He went mad. He flew into a rage about me making arrangements to meet someone else – he thought I was "packing him off" to the pub so that I could look for other men.' Ruby pulls on her cigarette deeply. 'It was truly ridiculous, but the next day he said it was all because he loved me. He said that's not how he was, it was just the strength of his love for me that made him behave like this.' She shakes her head and laughs. 'I can't believe I fell for it.'

Ruby is quiet for a minute and then says: 'It was after that that the phone calls started. I just can't believe I didn't suspect him.'

'So what's going on with his marriage, then?' I ask.

'Well, I met with his wife – she called me. She wasn't stupid and she knew there was someone else. She said she needed to know who I was, so I agreed to meet her. She told me that she had also found someone else, that she was very happy, and that I could "have" Jake if I wanted him. Stupidly I thought this would change things, even after the phone calls. I thought we could fix it. I saw him that night and I said that nothing could stop us now, not now that his wife had found someone else. It was like exploding a grenade. He stormed out in an absolute panic and I didn't hear from him for three days. When he did finally get in touch, it was all sweetness and light, but he said he was staying with his wife for the sake of the children. I finally realised he wasn't leaving her, ever.'

This is interesting: Jake was just as determined to continue controlling his wife and keep that relationship intact as he was about controlling Ruby and keeping that relationship intact. This wasn't all about love: it was about control and possession. He went into a full stage five escalation response when he thought his wife had someone else, just the same as he did with Ruby when he had failed to involve himself in the mortgage and thought she would leave.

'So what's happening now?' I ask. 'Has he gone?'

'He's still calling, but I refuse to take his calls. Sometimes he sits outside my house for hours. He's been through my bins, and he even broke into my locker at work. The worst thing was when I needed to change my front door. I was struggling to do it myself and he just turned up and said he would help me. I know I shouldn't have, but I let him and we were chatting. Then as soon as the door was off, he refused to put on the new one. He said it would stop me going out!'

'So he's not leaving his wife, but he's not leaving you, either,' I say. It is less a question than a statement.

'Maybe,' says Ruby. 'But I'm leaving him this time. I reported him to the police and to work. I think it'll stop now, as he might lose his job.'

*

Stalking and coercive control are twin behaviours: very often where there is one, there is the other. If stalking is thought of as any monitoring or tracking of a person, you can see how common it might be for a dominating individual, who wants to control someone else, to use it. Stalking becomes a means through which you gather intelligence. However, it can also be used to frighten someone, impose yourself on them and manipulate their daily activities.

There is a huge array of modern technology available these days to track and monitor people. I regularly lecture on stalking and one day, as an exercise, a student brought in a range of these items, dumping them on the bench in front of me. 'There you are,' he said. 'I got all these for less than a fiver each!' There was a pen, a mobile phone, an electrical plug, a memory stick, a car plug, and other similar items. All were monitoring devices that record sound or images, disguised as everyday items.

I sometimes work with the stalking advocacy organisation Veritas, which has a specialist cyber-stalking service: they advise people never to share their phone PIN with anyone, even a partner. Someone only needs brief access to your phone to install a wealth of hidden software that will send all of your texts, emails and so on to their phone without your knowledge, or track your every move.

*

When Gina separated from Fergus, he started following her, breaking into her home with a key he had kept, sending taxis and pizza deliveries; he damaged her car and she became frightened.

This was not simply about intelligence gathering or tracking; it was about fear and gaslighting. Fergus let Gina know *someone* had been in her home; he didn't do any damage when he was in there, but he would move things around.

He changed things very slightly but noticeably in her home, so she would question how, or even whether they had been moved. This is destabilising. The damage to her car made Gina feel she was being targeted, but it was only when she started putting things together, and recognising them as related, that she called it stalking. Sometimes giving something a name helps give the happenings some meaning, and therefore some structure.

It is clear to see the escalation in concerning behaviours in the cases of Karl, Vincent and Simone. Karl, predictably, increased the severity of the violence he used and the menace of his threats. Vincent veered between multiple methods to try and win back control. Simone started a long campaign of monitoring and tracking, and increased her suicidal threats.

The escalation stage is telling and is seen in many other situations where murder may be an outcome. I remember analysing the behaviours of Thomas Hamilton for a TV programme. He was the man who shot and killed sixteen children and a teacher at a school in Dunblane, Scotland, in March 1996. Hamilton had become enraged at being challenged about his behaviours around children. One particular example of his escalating behaviour in the period leading up to the murders struck me as significant: he had started writing letters of complaint about his perceived maltreatment to various individuals, and increasingly to people with power and status, culminating with a letter sent to the queen.

Though there will not always be patterns of escalation as clear as those exhibited by some of the cases here, there is often a ramping up of control to frighten or coerce the victim back into line. Even where there is no separation, there is frequently the suspicion that the trigger may cause one. Not all controlling people who reach the escalation stage will progress further. One of three things tends to happen on reaching stage five.

Firstly, the relationship may be reinstated and everything circles back to stage three. This means the couple return to their relationship, overshadowed by coercive control. They may say they will change, but this is unlikely without strong and outside intervention. This circling around stages three, four and five is the story of many controlling relationships. It is the pattern my sergeant, all those years ago, was used to seeing, and it is still very common. This constant circling is often a sign that the victim cannot leave, and pressure is being applied to make separation difficult or impossible. Victims may appear happy when the relationship is reinstated after a trigger and escalation – but this is more about hope that things will change and their life will be made easier. Things rarely change and this circling can go on for years.

The second common outcome is that the relationship may stay broken, and the controlling person finally accepts the break-up and circles back around to stage one, looking for their next victim. They may tell their next victim stories about the messy break-up and their unreasonable and difficult ex, giving away their history. They do this because they are still angry about the separation and see themselves as a victim of an injustice, and/or to elicit sympathy so that they can start the manipulation.

The third, and more concerning outcome, is that neither of those things happens, and the person moves forward to stage six. Most people will not progress to this next stage, even though they will continue to harass and stalk their victims for a very long time. Where there are divorces and child-contact battles, the escalation is made almost legitimate under the cover of a 'bad break-up', and these certainly happen where both engage in unnecessarily adversarial behaviours. However, in many cases where there has been coercive control the next logical step to punish and control will be an ongoing campaign to cause hurt. Here the family courts become an arena where coercive control is not only continued, but the court becomes an unwitting participant.

If the trigger is not a separation, but some other form of life change – like financial ruin, for example – that cannot be resolved, there is a risk that homicide may be the outcome where death is seen as the only way out. Some controlling people will kill themselves, but may also kill their partner and children.

It is common for controlling people to refuse to either relinquish control of their family or partner, or even compromise: it is part of their personality profile. For some, no compromise will suffice, only winning. That might be because they are the type who splits the world into winners and losers, or that they feel they have suffered a great injustice in losing their entitlements. I do not argue that all bad break-ups are about coercive control – they are not. But where they are, there should be enough expertise in the court system to protect those subject to the abuse of controlling people. I talk more about the dynamics between a controlling person and a victim in court in a later chapter.

If matters progress to stage six, then this is a lot more concerning. Stage six is a time when the escalation no longer serves its purpose, and the controlling person has changed their thinking about their strategy.

6

Stage Six: A change in thinking

It was a single act that got Vincent's family talking, and it is only with hindsight that they recognise it as a sign that he was becoming much more dangerous.

When he realised that he was not getting Donna to change her mind, Vincent's behaviour changed. Suddenly the attempts to manipulate Donna seemed to stop and his family noticed that he appeared calmer. They did not think this was a relaxed calmness; they described it as almost sneering. They felt unnerved by it, not threatened or frightened, just unnerved.

It was the night before Vincent killed Donna that it happened, the single event that caused them all to talk. Donna's children, who were no longer living at home, each received a phone call from her.

'You'll never guess,' said Donna. 'We didn't watch *Corrie* tonight!'

'What? You're kidding. No way, that can't be right,' they both said.

'I didn't say anything to him,' Donna continued, 'but he was just smiling. It was weird.'

Failure to watch a beloved TV programme is clearly not ordinarily a sign that someone is about to become a murderer. But it was a talking point because Vincent had always been so insistent on this ritual, so when he wavered from it for the first time they could remember since the children were young, it felt unsettling.

Vincent had changed tack. It was not so much that he had altered the routine, it was just no longer necessary to observe it; it was no longer important or useful to him. He did not need to enforce that control; he did not need the alarm system because he had decided he was going to kill Donna.

Stage six is neatly summed up by Professors Russell and Rebecca Dobash, specialists in intimate partner violence and homicide, when they say that a strategy can change from attempting to keep a partner in the relationship to destroying them for leaving it. This captures the principle of a change in thinking perfectly: in most cases where the trigger is separation, the controlling person starts to believe that the victim must be destroyed to reinstate their status. This is the first real and critical change where homicide may become more a probability than a possibility. The change in thinking is not always easy to see, and it is those closest to the person who will be most likely to notice subtle differences. Sometimes it is only with hindsight that these things become very much clearer.

Vincent's family said that the most menacing aspect to his behaviour in this stage was his sneering smile. It was a smile only he knew the basis of. It would have been difficult to say to anyone that they felt unsafe because he was smiling strangely to himself. But when put into context, his changed demeanour took on a different meaning. It was a warning.

'I couldn't have hurt her, because I loved her. . .'

In 2005 the *Guardian* newspaper journalist Katharine Viner published the names of seventy-two women killed by a partner in a twelve-month period. I researched each of the cases to look at how they had been explained in the courts and media reports, and published these findings in *Murder, Gender and the Media: Narratives of Dangerous Love* (2012). Katharine Viner's list was the first time I had ever seen such cases collated – it was certainly never done formally at that time. Since then, others have taken on this work, collecting the names of women killed by their partners and publishing them. Karen Ingala Smith, CEO of the charity Nia, runs a project called Counting Dead Women (go to the website: it is shocking) and similar websites are being created across the globe, as awareness grows as to the scale of this issue.

In most of the seventy-two cases I looked at back then, the defences and explanations for the women's deaths were appalling. The worst examples occurred when lawyers argued to have murder charges reduced to manslaughter. For example, a man claimed that he spontaneously killed his wife because she was too drunk to go on holiday. However, it was also revealed that he had a significant history of cruelty, torture and violence towards her. After killing his wife, he left her dead in a chair in their shared flat and went on holiday on his own. In the papers and in court he was described as heartbroken at losing his partner; he was found guilty not of murder but of manslaughter.

In another case the judge said that the victim had kept a knife under her pillow 'for good reason' because she was so terrified of her former partner and his threats to kill her. The same judge went on to say that the victim had seriously provoked her killer on the day he killed her – with that very knife – when she mocked his sexual abilities. There was no evidence presented to prove these comments had been made, but the killer was believed. I find it astonishing that someone who was so terrified that they kept a knife under their pillow would also feel confident enough to taunt the man about his sexual prowess.

Court arguments and decisions do not happen in a vacuum. Lawyers are well versed in what arguments are likely to succeed; they need that barometer of cultural and societal feeling to try and predict what juries will find plausible. What I found from my research was that courts, investigators, journalists and others really do seem to believe that these homicides are 'spontaneous', having been provoked by the victim. There has not been any serious *mainstream* challenge to this narrative for far too long.

*

When I first heard about Nancy's case I felt an immediate sense of outrage that so many murders are being justified in these ways. There seemed to be no real belief that certain homicides were in any way pre-planned or predetermined. Through conversations with Nancy's family I was able to establish definite evidence of a stage-six switch in thinking, where a decision had been made to kill when power was lost.

Nancy was a compassionate woman working as a medical professional, and she had recently been diagnosed with cancer. She knew her marriage was in a bad state – knew it was dangerous for her, in fact – and after years of fear and control, she had decided to tell her husband Angus that she was leaving him. 'I want a divorce, Angus,' she had said to him, quietly and firmly.

She told her family that he stood silently staring at her for what seemed like ages. Nancy wished he would say something so she would know what she would be dealing with, at least for the moment. Would he be angry? Would he cry? Would he just laugh at her? She said she began to feel light-headed.

Angus finally broke the silence. 'You don't get to make that decision,' he said calmly. He turned and left.

'So that's how it is,' she thought. Then, thinking on his last words to her, the panic set in. She called her family; she now knew she was in danger. 'He's going to kill me,' she told them.

Nancy knew what Angus was capable of. The years of menace, control and sexual abuse left her in little doubt. Whether she could make anyone believe her was another matter. But Nancy's family absolutely believed her.

A letter arrived for her the next day, a long, sad, but disturbing letter:

> My wife Nancy, you are the most wonderful woman, a caring mother and beautiful person. I have treated you very badly over the years, and you did not deserve this, I should have been different. I know I was wrong, and I will forever regret the things I did to you. I am going to end it. You will be free of me.

This had the look of a suicide note, Angus expressing remorse for the years of abuse he had put Nancy through. Maybe.

Suicide threats from controlling people in such a situation are a concern, but they are also quite common. Some of these will be real: the person may intend to take their own life, but in cases where there is coercive control it is prudent to consider them veiled homicide threats. When death has entered the conversation, it is indicating a very final view of things.

Nancy instinctively knew this; she realised things had escalated. She did not believe Angus was remorseful; she knew him too well. This was just the first salvo in what was going to be a single-minded and determined war.

He had not got the response he was trying to elicit: Nancy did not return to him, and neither did Angus attempt suicide. The suicide threat was probably an attempt to force the relationship back into his hands, though I don't believe the threat was a hollow one. Suicide was on his mind, but not as a solitary act. His show of remorse was, actually, in Angus's head, Nancy's last opportunity to change her mind – her final chance to make things right. He probably thought he was being fair, giving her a last chance. With all else failing, it was now that the death threats and the stalking began.

Nancy remained certain Angus would try to kill her. So certain she went to the police, panic-stricken, begging for help. The police saw Angus as more of a threat to himself than anyone else.

It is quite possible that Angus had had a change in thinking between the suicide threat and the death threats, going from one plan (to get Nancy back) to the final plan (to kill her). Some experts call this 'last-chance thinking', but it is not widely acknowledged. It has been described and identified for many years in other types of homicide and is talked about much more widely in the context of stalkers; as most stalkers are former intimate partners, there is a strong link.

Angus's next letter was not about how wonderful Nancy was, but what a 'bitch' she was and how she 'deserved to die' for taking everything away from him – all his entitlements. His letter pretended to say one thing, but meant quite another.

Angus maintained contact with his children and although they did not trust him, and believed him capable of hurting their mother, they still saw him. There is a belief that when two people separate the rage is confined and does not present a threat to others. This belief was perfectly articulated by a judge in the family courts talking to a woman in another case, who was being relentlessly stalked, harassed and threatened by her former husband. They were having battles over child contact. He said to her: 'Madam, it's not the children he hates, it's you.' This is to entirely misunderstand coercive control and the threats it produces. This behaviour is a campaign, and like most campaigns it has a purpose and a plan. The plan is often rigid and takes priority over anything and everything, and this makes it dangerous for all those in the eye of that storm, including children.

On the day Angus killed Nancy, he got access to her through his children. He went to pick them up in his usual access arrangements. He manipulated a situation where he got inside the house and, for the first time since their split, was in a room with Nancy alone. The children were in the house. Nancy knew that this was the day, and she called the police in a panic. That call recorded her death and, very sadly, those of her children. Angus also killed himself at the scene.

This was not necessarily exactly how Angus had planned things to happen. We know this because he left evidence of what the plan actually was. He had been forming a plan for some months; he had put together a 'murder kit' and was looking for an opportunity. There are some clues that gain significance only with hindsight. The change in tone after that first suicide note, where Angus switched from begging for forgiveness, to a far more sinister choice of words, and implied death threats. This should set off the alarms: it is a clear change of tack. Angus took three months to carry out his plan, and during that time the harassment and stalking of Nancy never stopped.

The calm before the storm

When Vincent had his change in thinking, he appeared calmer, smirking. He altered his routines and though these changes were noticed, they were not seen as dangerous. Simone changed: she too became calmer, as if the rage was more directed. Karl, on the other hand, seemed to get more angry, more reckless and more determined.

Devin made an almost instant decision to kill his girlfriend. He heard her talking to a friend about her plans to leave him. He was seething and that anger remained. Over the course of the day he went out and purchased a knife with the fixed intent that he would stab her with it. He hid it in his jacket and waited, as they had arranged to meet later in the day to go shopping together. It was at that meeting, in the middle of the town, as they talked, that Devin suddenly pulled out the knife and stabbed her in front of everyone. He kept stabbing and stabbing, way past the point that she died, just as Vincent had done. She was definitely frightened of Devin, and she knew he was dangerous, but I do not think she knew he intended to kill her on that day, unlike Nancy, who did know.

The changes at stage six are subtle but noticeable. Sometimes the person will actually tell friends of their decision. This is more common than you might think.

*

Elliot Turner told his friends that he intended to kill his former girlfriend, seventeen-year-old student Emily Longley;

he even told them how he planned to do it. It was reported that he asked them if he could practise strangling on them – his friends did not think he was serious. He was convicted of murder, having strangled Emily to death in his bed in his parents' home in Bournemouth in 2011.

Threats of suicide and threats to kill are not necessarily idle; both could signal a future homicide in this context and should be taken seriously every time. Some will be very specific and may get more specific over time. Elliot Turner said he intended to strangle Emily: that is specific and at the very least indicates he had pictured the assault in his head. He had decided to kill her and felt confident in telling his friends. It is quite possible that when they did not openly challenge him, he interpreted that as confirmation there was solidarity.

A bereaved family I was interviewing showed me a quite lengthy suicide note left by a man who killed himself, his wife and his four children. On the face of it, his words suggest remorse and sadness: he describes his victims as good people. But, much like Angus's note, this was a device to outline why he felt the murders had been 'necessary', a kind of logical explanation. When this case first hit the headlines, the killer was painted as tragic rather than determined, and feeling depressed more than justified. Those initial assumptions about him were fundamentally misleading. He did not go and kill his wife and children in a spontaneous fit of despair or melancholia. He was logical, organised, determined. Murder, he decided, was the answer and he carried that out on a day and time he had selected with reference to no one but himself. To escape the humiliation of an impending and irreversible life change, he decided to kill his wife and their children, so they would never find out, then he would kill himself. There was no negotiation. Once the decision was made he felt more in control and empowered.

In the period before the murders his behaviour changed, but not in any way that raised questions. These subtle changes were noticed afterwards. The trigger in this case was an imagined separation: he said to a friend he feared his wife would leave if she found out about an impending catastrophe of his making.

First, he moved the furniture around in the main living room – the victim's sister noticed this. Second, he had always been friendly with his wife's family and had never caused arguments or problems. They saw the victim and her children regularly, but never on her own, never without him. Suddenly one evening, he dropped his wife off to visit her mother and he left the two women to talk for a couple of hours before coming back to collect her. This hadn't happened before. Her mum mentioned it to her other daughter on the phone: 'He just left us alone together,' she said. 'He's never done that.'

'It's weird,' her daughter replied. 'But when I went round there yesterday he had moved the furniture. The furniture's been in the same place for twenty years. . .'

On their own these two things would not perhaps seem significant. They suggest, however, that something was changing, something in him. He had always been a dominant and controlling man, though not outwardly violent, and he followed routines; his in-laws thought he was a bit 'tightly wound', but never questioned it.

The murders were meticulously planned: there was an order to them and aspects that were designed to make sure he was not interrupted. His children were silenced before they were killed in a way that was brutal and cruel; the furniture had been moved to make sure he could maintain an element of surprise. He had always planned to kill himself, and he did this after writing his suicide note.

This man was avoiding losing face, losing status. He did not want his family to witness any humiliation he might suffer, and he did not want his wife to leave him. His wife and children had no say and no opportunity to support him through any difficulties he might suffer. His character was such that everyone had to die to protect his ego.

*

If the eight stages of the Homicide Timeline were better known and more clearly recognised, then we would be in a better position to spot changes earlier and maybe take steps to protect people.

This is a view supported by Rachel Williams. Rachel is a remarkable woman. Her violent and controlling husband went through all the eight stages and she can track his behaviour across each and every one. In the final stage he walked into her place of work with a gun and shot her, leaving her seemingly dying on the floor. He then fled the scene and hanged himself.

Though severely injured, Rachel survived. She now campaigns for the safety of victims of coercive control, stalking and domestic abuse, and runs a charity called Stand Up to Domestic Abuse (SUTDA). She can see stage six in her husband's behaviour quite clearly now. In the days before he attempted to kill her, he started to 'clear things up' in his life; this suggests he had always planned to kill himself as well as her. It was Rachel's husband who went to an ex-girlfriend and apologised for his abuse and then rehomed his dogs. By this stage he had reached a decision about how he was going to resolve his issues; his thinking had changed. He had made his decision and he knew he was going to kill Rachel and himself. Things did not go according to plan for him, and Rachel survived. A desperately tragic outcome of this murder attempt and suicide was that Rachel's sixteen-year-old son killed himself shortly afterwards. The victims of domestic homicide may extend beyond the intimate partner, as many cases show.

7

Stage Seven: Planning

One day at a police headquarters, I was talking to a detective. I had been training officers in risk assessment and we were having a follow-up meeting and discussing cases and other things. 'Look at this,' she said, handing me a small pile of photographs. 'You will find this really interesting.'

I took the photographs and shuffled through them. They were police evidence images and showed a number of items arranged tidily on top of a table. There were, among other things, rolls of duct tape, knives, cable ties, bin liners, a blindfold, plastic gloves, a gag, bleach, handcuffs, rope, twine, matches and a hammer. This was a murder kit.

'Can you believe it?' the detective said. 'This is what was in the boot of this bloke's car when we arrested him.'

We both looked at the assortment of items, recognising immediately that a murder had been prevented. A good feeling, but also terrifying.

The man who had put this kit together had recently separated from his wife. He had been stalking her and the police were aware of his activities. On this particular day she had called the police to report that he was outside her house watching her again. The police decided to arrest him and as part of that arrest they searched his car. Thank goodness they did. Angus also had a murder kit in his car when he killed

Nancy. What we do not know in either case is when those kits were put in the cars. They could have been there for ages, just waiting for an opportunity.

A murder kit is quite solid evidence of intent and planning, and when they are found they are tangible and may be difficult to defend. Other signs of planning may be more hidden and need to be uncovered.

Planning is a contentious issue, because if we accept that most of these killers plan their murders, we are again accepting that the crime of passion is a myth. If you plan, you are not just 'losing it' or reacting to a 'red mist' that allegedly comes down in an instant. You have had time to be rational, to think about what you are doing, and to make a decision. Regardless of pace, planning means intent to at least harm someone, whether those plans are formed over a year, weeks or hours. Some will plan only how and when they will commit the murder, like Vincent; some will wait for an opportunity to present itself; some will plan exactly how they will do it and prepare in advance, like Angus; some will plan not only the murder, but how they will get away with it. The average length of time between a separation and a homicide is just over a month.

Vincent decided when, where and how he would kill Donna; we know he was planning for at least a week. He did not set up an elaborate alibi or escape plan. So convinced was he that he was justified and so fixated on committing his crime that it did not occur to him to plan for the aftermath. Karl planned to seek Bonnie out and beat her as he had always done. He just chanced his arm that he could talk his way out of trouble with the police, as he had done so many times before. Simone may have spent many months planning the killing and her defence.

Iain Lawrence, a former pilot, made and carried out elaborate plans to kill his estranged wife Sally in a car crash. He somehow managed to get Sally in the car and drove it into a tree at over fifty miles an hour. As he intended, he survived and Sally was killed. The police investigated the accident as suspicious. Forensic evidence showed that the car had been driven at the tree, the brakes had not been applied, Sally's airbag had been disabled, and her seatbelt had been unclipped just before impact. There was evidence that the passenger airbag had been turned off six times prior to the collision, and this was suggested by police investigators to be test runs.

There are definitely those who plan to get away with murder, and unfortunately some who do. Robert Trigg, a former chef from Worthing, killed two partners by staging their deaths. In this case one of the families had to fight for five years to get the police to recognise the fact that their daughter had been killed by Trigg and had not, as he claimed, simply died in her sleep.

It is my experience of working on cases – be it police investigations, coroner's inquests or death reviews – that often professionals cannot, or will not, accept that something sinister has happened. I worked with one family to get an investigation into their daughter's death: it took over five years, but police have now declared that they should have investigated in the beginning and that the woman was in fact murdered by her partner. I am currently working on a number of such cases. The narrative and tone are starting to change, and I see many powerful and influential campaigns that are having a real impact. There is more willingness now among professionals to be curious and to look deeper. Sometimes we have to suspect something is wrong to be able to unearth the evidence: we sometimes 'have to believe before we can see'.

The death of Antoine Denis in Kent in 2010 is a simple example. The police attended a call for a sudden death and found a man lying on his back in his living room with no apparent injuries and no suspicious circumstances. The police believed that the man, in his mid-sixties, had died of natural causes, and the undertakers were called to remove his body. When the undertakers arrived and picked up Mr Denis to move him, they found blood and a knife in his back. The evidence of foul play was there, but not the belief that it might be. There are many factors that can blind us to the facts. We may make assumptions about the victim. Institutional racism played its part in the investigation, and in cases I have looked at, sexist assumptions can protect killers, as can assumptions we make about drug taking, sexuality or lifestyle.

Agatha Christie once said that if you want to get away with murder, kill someone who is expected to die. A woman contacted me recently to look into the death of her sister, who had been terminally ill. There was some compelling evidence that she had been starved just prior to her death, but it is very difficult to get people to listen, much less to act, especially in such circumstances. Too often the easiest explanation is accepted. I have seen cases staged to look like suicide, or to look like a burglary, a robbery or an argument. All were cases that on closer inspection had evidence available to raise strong suspicion. If that suspicion isn't raised until years afterwards, or after the opportunity for a forensic post-mortem has passed, the evidence to support a prosecution may be lost for ever.

Killers are not always sophisticated in their schemes and often look up information on the internet to help them plan their murders. Searches such as 'how to commit the perfect murder' and 'how to kill someone' are not uncommon. Some plans are more straightforward than others. Vincent, for example, decided at some point in the days or weeks before killing Donna that he would stab her to death. He decided it would be in the car park. He had no plans to try and evade capture, so there were no plans to dispose of Donna's body. It was a simple plan, but no less determined. At the other end of the spectrum is Angus, who meticulously mapped out how he was going to murder Nancy for over a year, although even then things did not entirely follow the plan.

The length of time between deciding to murder, and a murder happening, has been the subject of some disagreement in the legal system. It used to be that the provocation had to be immediately before a killing to claim provocation as a partial defence. This was challenged to take account of victims of domestic violence who might retaliate in significant fear when they felt it was safer to do so. A pivotal case is that of Kiranjit Ahluwalia, who set her husband on fire as he slept, hours after he had grabbed her hair and pushed a hot iron onto her face. Kiranjit had experienced almost a decade of horrific coercive control, underpinned by cruel violence, and she had tried to leave many times, but her husband always found her and dragged her back. She said she did not intend to kill him, only to incapacitate him – she poured petrol over his feet and set fire to them on the night in question, so as to give her time to escape the house safely with her children. Her husband later died of his injuries and Kiranjit was convicted of murder. She served just over three years before she successfully had her conviction reduced to manslaughter on appeal.

In legal terms, the time to plan and think is significant in considering intent to kill and culpability. It is important to unearth this evidence, especially as it does often exist. More important, perhaps, is the fact that this evidence often exists before the murder, and that may give great opportunities for prevention if such planning can be discovered before someone is killed.

When Devin decided to kill his partner, the intent and planning played out over just a few hours. Some argue this is short enough to be passionate. I disagree. Devin, and others like him who kill over such a short time span, still make plans and still act on them. They aren't grabbing the nearest weapon in a fit of anger.

Edith and Walter

One of the more controversial cases I have analysed is that of Edith and Walter. It is a case that divided people and revealed the most profound differences in the ways we think about relationships and control.

Edith and Walter had been married for over fifty years. They had four grown-up children and were both retired and living in a comfortable home on the Norfolk coast with no financial concerns. They had grandchildren living locally. Walter and Edith had a strong circle of friends and socialised together regularly. No one had ever seen them fight or argue together and Edith had never disclosed any violence to her friends that we know of. Their children had never expressed any concerns about their parents' relationship. Anyone looking at this picture of Walter and Edith's life wouldn't think there was anything to worry about.

One morning Edith and Walter were both found dead in the home they had shared for many decades. A friend who had called round to see them on a prearranged visit was surprised when no one answered the door. She was concerned because Walter and Edith were always at home in the mornings. She knew the key was always under the plant pot, so she took it and went in. She called out to Edith, and climbed the stairs, calling her name over and over. She was horrified to find Edith lying on her back on the floor of her bedroom. She had terrible head injuries and there was a lot of blood. Walter was in the garage in the car; he had used the exhaust fumes to kill himself.

Naturally, the community was shocked and distressed by the news. The first thing that came to mind was a burglary gone wrong. Had someone broken in and been challenged by the couple? It transpired very quickly from the police investigation, however, that Edith had been murdered by Walter, brutally and violently. He had then gone to the garage, sat in their car and killed himself. The biggest question for everyone was why – why, after fifty years of a seemingly happy marriage, did Walter do such a thing? And why in such a brutal and terrible way? People who knew them, and even the press, speculated that Walter had 'just snapped' – that he was suffering from some mental illness and it had completely changed his personality and rationality.

It was my job to unfold the mystery of why Walter did what he did. The police had established that Walter was responsible, but no one really knew the motivation. That is not to say that the police did not have strong suspicions. The first person I spoke with about this case was the senior investigating officer. He was an incredibly insightful and experienced detective, and was very helpful in briefing me about the background and the facts. As I sat in the police station looking through the case file, he said: 'I knew what it was straight away. You get a feel for these things. As soon as I walked into the kitchen and opened the cupboards, the hairs on the back of my neck stood up.'

'What did you see?' I asked him.

'Neat rows, everything in order. Every cupboard, every drawer. I knew then – I knew what this was about.'

His comments had a familiar ring. It is certainly not an offence to have a neat kitchen. Neither is it a problem to be overly ordered and obsessive about lists and rows and categories. But sometimes, in some circumstances, it is part of a much bigger jigsaw. It sometimes suggests a very controlling and controlled personality. The order and neatness was such that it was clear that it had some meaning for Edith and Walter. My concerns were further raised when I started to look deeper into their relationship.

Edith and Walter had met over fifty years before, when Edith worked in a shop. A quiet and relaxed young woman living a very ordinary life, she was popular and easy to know. This is how people remembered her. Walter swept her off her feet and within a year of meeting they were married with their first child born.

Walter, in contrast, was not described as easy-going; his friends considered him to be anything but. They described him as being argumentative and dominant. He always had to win the arguments he started, and was quite loud and pushy. Many people said they just let him win arguments because being right was so important to him. Walter was also considered to be a bit thin-skinned and did not take criticism well. He was not good with challenge. His friends knew this about him, so were careful not to wind him up. They seemed to like him and none of these things seemed to threaten the friendships.

When commenting on Walter and Edith's relationship, friends said things that I have heard so many times, especially about older couples. The comments had a familiar ring. It was said they never argued and were always together, that they were 'devoted' to each other. One thing that they all agreed on, and was mentioned by everyone, was their predictability. 'You could time your watch by them' was a repeated (and affectionate) comment. Friends told of Walter and Edith following strict routines. However, on close inspection this was way beyond what anyone would think was comfortable or normal. Edith and Walter had a timetable that never varied and was incredibly detailed. Every activity had a day, and a time to be started and finished. On one occasion a friend said that the local supermarket did not have Walter's particular brand of tea. He made a loud and aggressive complaint, far in excess of what would have been appropriate. He could not tolerate his routines being changed or disrupted in any way. Edith was known to be far more relaxed, which suggests that she followed the routines to keep Walter happy. These were Walter's routines.

This picture of their life raises some red flags. They started their relationship in a time when Walter's way of doing things could be imposed without anyone considering that strange or wrong. This was the way of things in the culture at the time. Men were not only justified in being in control, but were encouraged to be that way. Edith very probably went along with Walter's quirks and demands, seeing it as the way of things. It is highly likely, given the severity of the routines, that they had special meaning for Walter, which suggests that he would have a very negative response to anyone not complying with his requirements or the routines being disrupted.

This need for control over every aspect of his and Edith's life was probably very deep-rooted. Edith would have learned quite early what the consequences of disrupting or challenging Walter's routines would be. Given the culture she was living in, and her relaxed approach to life, it is not surprising his requirements dominated her life. But that is not to say she did not experience the repercussions of not complying. It is probable that she learned through trial and error how to keep life on an even keel. It only takes one shock, one lesson, to set the tone for the future. Edith and Walter's lifestyle, dominated by routine, is not at all unusual in cases of coercive control, especially in older couples. I have seen many cases, so, like the detective, I was not surprised to hear about this.

This presents us with a conundrum about coercive control. If Edith was following the routines consensually, does this make the situation abusive? Whatever your position, it does not reduce the risk should Edith suddenly decide that she does not like her life with Walter, and wants to separate. We do not really know how Edith felt because no one ever asked her, and the balance of power in the house was normalised as sitting with Walter. We do know they never argued and Edith was always accompanied by him when out.

This could suggest that arguing was not allowed, and neither was Edith allowed much freedom. That is the case for many women, especially of Edith's age group. A clear problem is that controlling personalities and behaviours can be hidden in a culture that normalises such control. Walter's quite high-risk anxieties and demands were indistinguishable from more normal expressions of the masculine 'head of the household' role, taking in the context of this relationship having started at a time when such things were unquestioned.

We also know that a few months before Edith's murder, things started to change in Walter's life. Edith began to get ill. Her illness meant there was some disruption to Walter's routines. Edith could not always manage to be there at the right times, doing the right things. Doctors and nurses started to take some of the decision-making away from Walter. He began to get very irritable. He became more argumentative in the final weeks, and when he found that there were some things in his life that would have to change irrevocably, he started to become incredibly difficult, angry and unpredictable. Their friends talked of the shift in his personality as he tried to grapple with the changes. Edith confided in her doctor and her best friend before her murder that she was finding him impossible to live with. She even said that she wanted to leave her marriage. After fifty years she said she had had enough.

We know that they had started to argue and Edith was asserting herself more. We also know that he made plans to kill her. He had started sorting out all his financial affairs and made a new will. He planned to kill himself after killing her.

The murder of Edith was brutal and violent. He beat her with a hammer and a broom. There was evidence that she tried to defend herself from the attack. This was not a mercy killing, and this was not about love.

Putting together the jigsaw revealed that there were problems in the marriage, but maybe not what anyone would recognise as worrying. The routines and rituals were in place for a reason. The fact that friends said that they never argued is potentially a sign that one of the partners is avoiding any kind of argument or challenge for fear of the consequences. Friends also said that they were always together. Sometimes this indicates that one of the couple has no freedom to have interests that do not include the other. The implications of Walter's lifelong need to micro-control his and Edith's lives were never challenged or acknowledged. Why did he need so much control? Why were the consequences of not having control so severe for him? Should this have been identified as a problem much earlier? If it had been, it could have saved Edith's – and Walter's – life.

It was speculated by many that Walter must have suffered some mental illness and killed Edith because of this – a very convenient but empty explanation. It may be easier to point at the smoking gun and have half an explanation than dig deeper and face some uneasy truths. Mental illness is often cited as a cause for murder. It is true that some killings of partners or children may be carried out during a psychotic episode. Psychosis is sometimes obvious and is a clear defence. However, mental illness where psychosis is not present cannot be a cover-all explanation. It doesn't help us prevent such murders happening in the future.

Similarly, drug and alcohol misuse are sometimes considered explanations for murder. Though they often exacerbate issues, drug and alcohol misuse are not necessarily causal, and where we cite them as causal, but coercive control is in evidence, we do not learn anything, and we defend the homicide.

This was the case in the death of Kasia, which was found to have been caused by illicit drug toxicity, despite her having no history of drug misuse. There was bruising to her neck caused by being held in a headlock, and also bruising to her mouth. It was decided that she had taken an accidental overdose during a sex game. Her partner, a known drug user, had just found out she was leaving him. There was a significant history of coercive control underpinned by violence known by the police, but still she was said to have caused her own death. Anyone with any forensic knowledge or even curiosity may see the evidence of headlock and the bruising to her mouth as at least suggestive that there had been forced ingestion of the drugs. But this was not followed up. It has been now, but it took a very long time.

We are learning so much more with the more searching questions that are being asked. Even if people do not 'like' the idea that these homicides are planned, the evidence shows that many of them are, and that they are planned after a trigger event.

I was recently looking into the death of a young woman who had three small children. She had been in a relationship with a controlling person and had recently separated from him. The report came in to the police that she was a missing person. The senior investigating officer suspected the former partner, and instead of leaving it as a missing person enquiry, he upgraded it to a homicide investigation immediately, having already investigated the former partner for domestic abuse and coercive control. He explained to me that he would rather be wrong and the woman turn up safe and well than miss the chance to collect the evidence, find the woman's body, and secure her killer's conviction. This officer was experienced, he knew about these homicides, and he told me that the whole case had followed my eight-stage timeline. Tragically she did not turn up safe and well. Shortly after she went missing they found her body, buried in a field nearby. They also got a conviction of murder against her former partner.

8

Stage Eight: Homicide and/or suicide

I was researching Jack the Ripper some years ago. It was a project that affected the way I think about murder and its victims. I had come across a photograph of the gravestone of Catherine Eddowes, one of the five generally agreed victims. On it were the words 'here lie the remains of Catherine Eddows [*sic*]... buried 8th October 1888', and then in large letters, very nearly as large as the letters spelling her name, were the words 'Victim of Jack the Ripper'. I was horrified. Who decided to define this woman's entire life, and then her death and memory, with a tabloid-generated pseudonym of the unknown man who killed her? Would she have wanted that? Did her family want that? Should we want that?

Too often there is a voyeuristic interest in the killers, and the victim can be for ever memorialised as a chapter in the life of their killer. The taking of a life can become the taking of an entire history or legacy.

Many of my students have an enduring interest in murderers, especially serial killers, and I always try to explore with them why that is. Some have come to find criminology interesting through true crime documentaries and books, which have certainly raised the profile of many homicides and expanded what we think we know about them, and the questions we ask. There is far less interest, however, in hearing about victims or their stories, even though it is the victim's perspective that can reveal the most damning and helpful information. It is also the case that many people interested in true crime will not ever have experienced how deeply disturbing such crimes are. It is quite different to read a description of a crime scene than to walk through one.

I remember when I was on an attachment to what was then called the CID, receiving a call to attend an armed robbery in progress. I was with a colleague, and on hearing the call we both looked at each other in alarm for a split second and I felt the fear rising in both of us. A bank was being held up and the offenders had shotguns. We were unarmed, in plain clothes, and in an unmarked car. Despite this we careered towards the bank and were in fact the first unit to arrive. It was the strangest experience. The evidence of their presence was everywhere, though the robbers had run from the scene. We pursued them, but we never caught up with them. Everything had changed in that bank in the space of a second. Ordinary things had become exhibits and evidence, and ordinary people had become witnesses to trauma, threat and terror. The atmosphere was anything but ordinary: it was sinister and heavy; it held the fragility of life and death and the potential for human wickedness.

All serious crime scenes have this, and I always wonder at how things might have played out had someone chosen to behave differently. You have to decide to pull a trigger and shoot someone, or to lift a knife to stab someone. Intimate partner homicides are particularly disturbing because the choices made are too often excused, and the horror minimised. When I first started studying them I was surprised. I had not realised the levels of violence – and by that

I mean I had an assumption that they were spontaneous acts of anger, largely unintentional, with minimal violence. I could not have been more wrong. These homicides often involve shocking levels of sustained violence – 'overkill'. This overkill suggests unyielding rage: there is rarely a single stab wound, shot or punch.

The various ways these homicides play out are complex. Sometimes children are the targets – killed as part of the plan; sometimes they are 'collateral damage' – the determination to kill the partner being so rigid that children do not matter and will be killed if they get in the way. Some homicides will be hidden; some will include the suicide of the killer; sometimes both the children and mother are killed, while other murderers focus on the children in order to create the most trauma for the mother. Most frequently the children are present and may witness the killing of their mother.

*

The very first time I went to visit a bereaved family was with Frank Mullane, founder of Advocacy After Fatal Domestic Abuse (AAFDA). I had first met Frank when I was researching a book about domestic homicide and had contacted him to help me understand the family and victim perspective, one of which I had hitherto had little experience. It was probably the most important meeting of my entire career, because it transformed the way I think about what can be done to try to stop these murders.

Up to that point I was fired up by a sense of outrage, which led me to see these injustices in isolation. Ironically, for one who had lost two close family members in such horrific circumstances, Frank seemed less angry than me. We both wanted things to change, but Frank was perhaps more alert to what anger could achieve and how. From talking to him I came to realise that professionals – people like police officers or social workers who make snap decisions under huge pressure and with little support – make flawed decisions, much of the time with good intentions. (There are also those who make deliberately damaging decisions, but I think they are in the minority.)

When Frank's sister, Julia, and nephew, Will, were murdered, following a long history of domestic violence, a whole host of poor decisions by professionals was uncovered that had made her less safe, and contributed to her ex-husband being able to execute his plan. None of the people who made the uninformed decisions intended for Julia or Will to be hurt. These decisions were predicated upon the truths hidden in a heavily flawed belief system. We need to dismantle those beliefs and replace them with facts.

That first bereaved family Frank took me to visit were very welcoming. I had a strong sense as I walked into their home of something horrific having been imposed on two unsuspecting, regular and lovely people. They had been about to retire when their daughter was murdered by her ex-husband. They had worked hard all their lives in physically demanding jobs and finally their time had come for some rest. Suddenly, literally overnight, they had lost their daughter in horrific circumstances and become full-time parents to three traumatised and effectively orphaned children. Their house did not automatically get bigger, and there was no extra money to accommodate this momentous change. The children had witnessed their father attempt to decapitate their mother in the family home; it was a bloody and disturbing crime scene even for the experienced professionals who attended it. The deep trauma inflicted on the children was something the grandparents had been largely left alone to deal with.

The children's mother had been planning to relocate closer to her family, having left her husband after years of coercive control. The judge, commenting at the end of the trial, said he considered the husband to be an extremely dangerous man and that he should be in prison for a significant amount of time. However, eleven years after the murder the man was serving his sentence in an open prison and was being considered for release. The grandparents have watched their grandchildren too scared to go upstairs alone, too scared to be in a room alone, just in case their father comes back. For me, unless this man has had his control issues robustly dealt with, there is the very strong possibility that he could behave in a controlling and dangerous way with his next partner when he is out and unsupervised and back at stage one of this timeline.

Some controlling people will go through all eight stages more than once. I always think that the murder of Angela Best in 2016 is one we should never forget. As I noted right at the beginning of this book, Theodore Johnson, Angela's long-term partner, was able to travel through the eight stages three times, killing three partners. The first time was in 1981, when he killed Yvonne Johnson – he was convicted of manslaughter after being described as a 'battered husband' by the judge. Johnson was able to manipulate the way he was perceived, and only served three years. Then, in 1993, he killed Yvonne Bennett after pleading 'diminished responsibility'. He was sent to a secure hospital and was released after two years. In 2016 he killed Angela Best, but this time, finally, he has been convicted of murder and sentenced to twenty-six years. It is outrageous that he was able to kill three partners, and that these crimes weren't even hidden. We all knew.

Recognising homicide and suicides

Research has found that between four and ten women who have recently suffered domestic violence kill themselves every week in the UK. Add to that the number of men in similar situations. The first conviction for manslaughter after a suicide was achieved in 2018. Forty-six-year-old Justene Reece killed herself as a result of intolerable and terrifying stalking by her ex-partner, who was sentenced to ten years in prison for manslaughter, stalking and coercive behaviour.

Suicide as a result of domestic abuse and coercive control is a problem, and the numbers are not fully recognised. The true number of intimate partner homicides, meanwhile, is also difficult to calculate for many reasons. There are those that are discovered, someone is found to be responsible and it is recorded officially as a homicide. Others are not recognised or recorded. Unfortunately, I have seen many deaths recorded as misadventure, accident, suicide, natural causes and so on, where more investigation was needed. So the number of homicides is higher than we think. Consider the case of a woman who was beaten to death in a relentless assault that lasted a couple of days. The official cause of death was given as GBH, rather than homicide, even though she died during the beating. Her family, who I have met, are still fighting the police, the courts, the pathologist and anyone else who cannot see the injustice. It is not a case of saying the evidence is not there, as it simply is. For instance, this man called the police and stated: 'I think I've killed my girlfriend.'

Experienced lawyers working on such cases tell me that pathologists do not always search with curiosity, even in full forensic post-mortems. Outcomes can vary greatly, depending on the individual professional's understanding of coercive control. I have seen for myself how some coroners or pathologists are more questioning and probing than others. In one now notorious case, a woman found with a head injury in a clear crime scene was said to have died from a heart attack. The pathologist refused to consider the context in which the heart attack had occurred, so the police had no homicide to investigate, despite wanting to. The man who caused the head injury, and potentially the heart attack, went on to kill three more women before he was convicted of murder. Generally, however, professionals throughout the criminal justice system are becoming more knowledgeable about such crimes. Bit by bit, the sands are shifting and the conversations are changing.

*

Two male celebrities have dominated global headlines in recent years after the deaths of their partners. One is the former American National Football League star O. J. Simpson; the other is South African sprinter Oscar Pistorius. It is a matter of public record in these two cases that both men had histories of serious coercive control underpinned by violence. In both cases, the public seemed split on whether they believed them to be guilty: both Simpson and Pistorius were excused, given sympathy and defended. Their trials did not end with straight murder convictions.

In the criminal courts O. J. Simpson was acquitted of the murder of his former wife, Nicole Brown Simpson, and her friend Ronald Goldman. He was then found culpable for their deaths in the civil courts. Simpson was known to be controlling and had used violence against Nicole; the police had been called in the past and he was known to be stalking her when she died. Having escaped criminal conviction, Simpson published a book called *If I Did It: Confessions of the Killer*, giving what he said was 'a hypothetical' description of the events – an extraordinary and incendiary thing to do. After Simpson was found culpable in the civil trial, it was decided that all proceeds from the book should go to Ronald Goldman's family so Simpson would no longer profit.

Oscar Pistorius was found guilty of murdering his girlfriend Reeva Steenkamp only after a second trial, and was sentenced to just six years. He was shown to have had a history of possessiveness, jealousy, violence and threat against intimate partners, and his management of Reeva Steenkamp's life was obsessive. He had used a gun to threaten girlfriends in the past and he had previously locked Reeva in his house. Though many hoped that these high-profile trials with worldwide audiences would stimulate debate and highlight awareness of coercive control and domestic violence, the focus quickly shifted from the victims to issues surrounding the accused, such as race and disability.

Similarly, in the now notorious 1974 case of 'Lucky' Lord Lucan, his disappearance has eclipsed the fact that he was excessively possessive and controlling, and was vengefully stalking his estranged wife just prior to the crimes.

Mick Philpott was also a man who gained some notoriety: the media interest in what was perceived to be his 'keeping two wives' in one home was significant and that 'nudge nudge' atmosphere stifled discussions around the horrific coercive control suffered by both 'wives'. There was also little interest in the fact that Philpott had tried to murder a former girlfriend and her mother by stabbing them multiple times. The former girlfriend had tried to leave and Philpott served just over three years of a seven-year prison sentence for this attack. There should have been serious concern around the situation of Philpott living with two women, not least of all because there were ten children living in that household with a man known to be violent and controlling.

Six of those children died in a fire set by Philpott in May 2012 in an attempt to punish one of his 'wives' when she left him, as he tried to make it look as if she had set the fire. Even when politicians decided both before and after the deaths to make some comment on Philpott, they did not talk about coercive control; instead they talked about so-called 'benefits culture' in a blindingly inept assessment of the murders. Conservative MP Ann Widdecombe famously went to stay with Philpott in 2007 as part of a documentary, *Ann Widdecombe Versus the Benefit Culture*, with the overriding message she wanted to give him being 'get a job'. His previous attempts to kill two women were not mentioned, probably in some agreement with Philpott, but production of the programme was more important than the horrific abuse and violence, and the real good that could have been done by making this story about coercive control, and not about 'benefits scroungers'. Harold Shipman, one of the world's most prolific killers, was also accused of coercive control and domestic abuse. Domestic abuse is not merely a series of fights between two people; it is a mindset and an inflexible and dangerous way of operating.

It is crucial that such homicides are accurately described and explained so that similar potential killers might be prevented in the future. Recently I worked with the UK charity Level Up on their campaign for a press code of conduct on reporting intimate partner homicides. Irresponsible reporting can have a variety of consequences – from misinforming the public about their safety, to victim blaming, to the unnecessary and traumatic defaming of deceased victims who have no voice. As a result of the campaign there are now guidelines, which were adopted by leading press regulators IMPRESS (Independent Monitor for the Press) and IPSO (Independent Press Standards Organisation) in 2019.* It will be interesting to see how widely they are followed and adopted.

* I would suggest that complaints about unfair or misleading reporting of these homicides should always be put in writing to the publication in question, especially as we now have a code for regulators and editors to refer to.

9

After homicide

A homicide does not end on the day of a murder. It is the beginning of an investigation, a coronial process, a trial, and maybe a death review. Children may be orphaned, and there is unimaginable pain to be endured by the victim's family – and probably the killer's family too. Much of my work begins after a murder has happened. Conversations about the aftermath are almost as important in altering narratives as those about spotting the danger signs.

After a murder the controlling person will invariably attempt to manipulate and control what others believe happened. Very often their control of the victim, now deceased, continues in the way they are presented after death. The controlling person will continue to influence the way others perceive the relationship: they do not care how the victim is remembered. They will try to make the victim appear culpable in their own death. This may be through, say, lying about the person's temperament, their mental health, their sexual activities, whether they loved their children. Where there has been travel through the eight stages, manipulation is all.

I recently opened an email marked 'urgent' from a police investigator requesting I look at a cold case. It had not been recorded as a homicide at the time of the victim's death, but evidence had come to light in the intervening years, arousing suspicion. The police had been looking at the eight stages patterning, along with new evidence, with a view to making an arrest. It was my job to look at the case history and assess the possibility of homicide, and also to give advice around interviewing the suspect and any witnesses. I am increasingly asked for my forensic opinion on intimate partner homicides, and also on high-risk cases where the victim is still alive. This is a positive sign that the complexities of both victim and perpetrator behaviours are beginning to be recognised and accepted. Identifying coercive control cannot be left to 'common sense'; we should recognise that the behaviours deviate from the norm and are worthy of scrutiny. The more the eight-stage timeline is part of everyone's understanding, the more such killers will be held to account, and the more we might be able to protect victims before the worst happens.

It is not only research and a more nuanced understanding of coercive control and stalking that has pushed this radical shift in thinking; it is the campaigning by families who have been bereaved through homicide. Many of the best and most effective charities and campaigns have been started by bereaved families: AAFDA, as I have mentioned, was started by Frank Mullane after the murders of Julia and Will Pemberton; PAS was started by Tricia Bernal after the murders of Clare Bernal and Rana Faruqui; the Suzy Lamplugh Trust was established by her family after the disappearance of Suzy Lamplugh; the Alice Ruggles Trust was started by Sue and Clive Ruggles after the murder of their daughter Alice; and the Hollie Gazzard Trust was started by Nick Gazzard after the murder of his daughter Hollie. Campaigning by Luke and Ryan Hart began after the murders of their mother and sister, Claire and

Charlotte Hart; SUTDA was started by Rachel Williams after she was shot by her husband and survived. Think also about the campaigning work of others bereaved: Doreen Lawrence after the murder of her son Stephen, or the families of the victims at Hillsborough football ground and Grenfell Tower. It is a fact that they campaign very hard, but it is sad that they have to.

The ingrained but often subconscious societal belief that some lives matter less than others has been a thread in many campaigns. The Black Lives Matter campaign, for example, has highlighted how such beliefs can and do create environments where some people are less safe, and their abusers systematically better protected, than others. It is something that should concern all of us, not only because we often assume we are higher up that hierarchy of who matters than we actually are. Wives and girlfriends are pretty low down when it comes to allegations of violence, homicide or sexual abuse from their partners: research has found that women who live with their abuser or killer have the lowest status as victims of domestic abuse. Women as a sex class have lower status than many of us imagine.

Male victims of control can also find themselves slipping down a victim hierarchy, especially if they are gay, or find themselves using defensive violence. Men also often believe they are in less danger than they might be: Simone's husband Henri is testament to that. The instinctive way we blame victims and attempt to share culpability is not helping anyone except a handful of determined killers.

As we have seen, children are also commonly victims, but largely silenced and carrying lifelong trauma. In one case I reviewed, the seventeen-year-old child of the victim intervened in an assault and killed the perpetrator of abuse. At the tender age of seventeen he found himself in court charged with murder. The jury in this case found him not guilty, but that is something that this young man will carry with him for the rest of his life. There are no guarantees how coercive control might play out, and who may be hurt in the perpetrator's campaign.

Trials and inquests happen after homicide and are an opportunity to find out what happened and why. But for families they can be frightening and disturbing events. I attended two inquests recently and in both cases I was disappointed. At one, organisations that had relevant information to present were represented by barristers. There were five of them. The family had no barrister, and neither could they afford one. In the second inquest, there were eight barristers representing organisations, and again the family had no money for such help. In both cases the barristers argued to block information being made public, block the family questions and block family witnesses. In no possible light can this be seen as fair or just, or a way to reveal the facts of the case. Coercive control is difficult enough to see sometimes, and if there are convoluted legal arguments further blocking the release of evidence, the whole process becomes ineffective and unfit for purpose.

I have been running a project I call 'Hidden Homicide'. We are researching sudden and unexpected deaths that have followed the eight-stage pattern, but have not been investigated, prosecuted or recorded as homicide. There are far more of these cases than you would imagine, and I am often contacted by bereaved families and professionals from across the world. The problem is not confined to the UK.

In my experience these sudden deaths are often simplistically assessed as non-suspicious, even where there are clear grounds for suspicion and families are arguing for an investigation. In some of these cases, which take years to progress, police have had to reinvestigate, and in some cases they have reversed their original decisions. It is heartbreaking for families to see suspects walk free, only to continue their abuse with their next partner. I think that, at the very least, if there is a history of coercive control or domestic abuse, a sudden and unexpected death should be investigated.

In one case I looked at, a young woman was found dead, surrounded by her bags and suitcases as she tried to leave. Her partner, who had a history of domestic abuse, said she strangled herself in the bed sheets by accident. In another case a woman was said to have stabbed herself to death, despite there being a child witness to the events who said otherwise; in another case the victim, who had already left a very abusive partner and was hiding from him, was found in her partner's room dead from a massive illicit drug overdose. She was not a drug user and her partner had said he was going to kill her and make it look like an overdose. The role of domestic abuse, violence and coercive control in a sudden death is not always assessed as relevant, and that has to change.

The idea of coercive control extending into the courtroom or an inquest is deeply troubling. A case in point is that of the murder of six-year-old Ellie Butler at the hands of her father, Ben Butler. At the trial Ellie's mother, Jennifer Gray, supported her husband. No one could understand why she had stood by him, protected him and lied for him in two separate trials.

I am going to talk about this case and the importance of recognising coercive control in the legal system, such as the coercive control and violence suffered by both Jennifer Gray and Ellie Butler before she died, and the possible impact of that abuse in a trial.

Ben Butler

Ben Butler had been convicted of seriously assaulting his daughter when she was just a few weeks old, fracturing her skull and, as a result, she was rightly removed from his care and the care of her mother.

Butler appeared more affronted than remorseful and decided to challenge that decision and regain custody. This may have been less because he was a loving father and more because he was controlling and needed to win his battle with the health services and the courts. And win he did. He manipulated the system and the professionals within it to such an extent that they quashed his conviction and returned the child to his custody, stating explicitly that there should be no stain on his character and that he was the victim of a miscarriage of justice. He knew he had got away with it, and his wife knew it too.

Ellie had been placed in the care of her grandparents at less than a year old after the assault. The little girl had only ever known life with them, but despite this she was returned to her parents.

At first, when he won his court battle, Butler looked like a hero, a man who had been wronged by the system, who had fought to regain custody of his child against the odds. Butler clawed back his status – and then some. He appeared on TV programmes with his partner Jennifer, Ellie's mother, to talk about his victory and the injustice that had spurred him on in his five-year battle. But within twelve months of that victory, little Ellie was dead, killed by Butler after he once again assaulted her, causing catastrophic head injuries.

This appalling homicide captured the heart and conscience of the nation: Butler's trial for Ellie's murder was highly publicised. Such was his confidence in his own abilities to beat the system a second time that he conducted his own defence. I was told by those there that he treated the courtroom as if it was his personal stage. Acting like a master of ceremonies, he seemed to bask in the adversarial nature of the proceedings and the allure of winning and taking back control. He told the jury that he was the victim of injustice, that he was being persecuted by the legal system.

Butler appeared to be a narcissistic and deeply unpleasant individual. Once you know that and accept it, the danger is easier to see, and it is no surprise that he killed Ellie. So why wasn't it seen earlier? If it had been, little Ellie might still be alive.

Jennifer Gray was married to Butler and living with him when Ellie was assaulted on both occasions, but was not present for either assault. She did, however, help Butler to try and cover up the assaults and she stood beside him in the court at the murder trial, a co-accused. She would not speak against him and presented a picture of their relationship together that, after some belated and overdue checks, was found to be patently untrue.

This was not an intimate partner homicide, but it could have been – Gray was at high risk. The assaults on Ellie happened in a setting of violent coercive control, and Butler was travelling through the eight stages. He was at stage one of the eight-stage timeline even before the first injury to Ellie, because he had a history of convictions for assault, both in the context of domestic abuse and random assaults on other men. It is also interesting that his relationship with Jennifer Gray started very quickly. She was pregnant within eight weeks of their meeting in a pub. There was also evidence, presented in the second trial, of domestic abuse and coercive control that put Butler at stage three. Gray denied there was any abuse, even in the face of strong evidence to the contrary. She supported him in his claims that he was a good father, and was not abusive, even though their daughter was dead by his hand.

People ask the question: *Why on earth would a mother behave in such a way?* It is a valid question and should have been given far more serious consideration in both trials. Though my following analysis of the situation may be challenging to read, it is important to look at the predicament in which Ellie's mother found herself. I do not attempt to defend her – far from it – but I do take a look at the crippling, paralysing effects of Butler's control and violence that left everyone in that household at risk of serious harm.

*

Evidence was presented in court that showed horrifying levels of coercive control, enforced through violence suffered by Gray and Ellie. Text messages, diary entries and web searches show the abuse. The following are three messages Gray (secretly) typed into an internet search engine when she was alone, prior to the murder of Ellie, which were revealed in court:

> My husband is a bully who beats me and tells me I'm ugly and fat and hurts me all the time.
>
> I wish I was dead because he hurts me so much and I can't escape. Nobody really cares about me any more.
>
> Urgent magic spell needed to stop him hurting me and make him sorry.

Gray was evidently feeling isolated and desperate. She was even reduced to searching for magic spells to try and change things, and this suggests she was isolated from other, more usual support networks. Coercive control deliberately isolates its victims, often cutting them off from outside influence and help.

I read through hundreds of text messages between Gray and Butler, which he thought had been deleted. It does not take advanced forensic skills to reveal their brutality. Gray said in court that they were not threatening, but were just his way of expressing himself. What does come across very clearly is the consistency of the type of messages. Butler is consistently threatening, abusive and controlling; Gray is consistently apologetic, placatory and desperate. The texts are not examples of simple arguing: they show brutal dominance and submission patterns. The sheer volume of these hundreds of messages show that they are not odd spats, but the way the relationship operated.

I have selected some messages to make my point. They are not the worst: I have deliberately chosen them to show the type of messages that are repeated time and time again.

Butler: Take Ellie walk streets. U aint coming here. . . . I'll maim you bitch.

Gray: I am shaking and been in tears. UR that hateful. I am not being mouthy. UR being terrifying and impossible... I really am trying to show U all the good stuff and stuff you want.

Gray was made to walk the streets, sometimes with toddler Ellie, when she displeased Butler, and had been locked out all night on some occasions. These texts show her trying to placate him. He had already manipulated the courts into thinking he was an exemplary father, and Gray had witnessed the amount of power he exerted in that process. He had proved to her he could beat the system and that he could win custody battles. The media presented him as a hero after the first trial; everyone was on his side. In begging and placating him she may have felt, at some level, that she was managing her safety and that of her children. There are messages and internet searches that talk of assaults and injuries, and it was found that Ellie had old trauma fractures after her death.

Internet search by Gray: Extremely swollen head on left side after trauma – symptoms for head swelling up and what to do.

Butler: You are dead when I come home slag.

Gray: I am telling you now, I am listening to you and this does not happen all the time Ben. Please do not leave me like this. Please come back.

People might question at this point why she didn't just leave. But let's also ask why, if he hated her so much and was so disgusted by her, why didn't *he* leave? Why didn't he – who

did have the power to walk away and was not living in fear –
just leave? It was because his insults and threats were not a
reflection of a wish to free himself from her, but more likely a
method to trap her with him.

> Butler: Cancel your hair [appointment] or take your kids
> there, but I'm not looking after them. Now fuck off you
> ugly bitch.

It may seem on first reading that Gray could just take
the children and go somewhere safe – and why would she
want him looking after them, anyway? We need to read more
into this. The outcome of the use of children is often a terror
that custody hearings may force children into situations that
only the victim seems to recognise as dangerous. Butler had
already won the most difficult of custody hearings. It is possible that Gray might have been standing by him, placating
him, *at least in part* to keep her children and herself safe. She
was possibly terrified that he could kill her or one of the children. Of course, that is exactly what happened. Because Gray
had stood by him and lied in the first trial, her testimony in
any future hearings could be considered suspect. She might
have had the very real fear that he would get custody. She
was backed into a corner. This is just a part of the complex
jigsaw of the web of control. But we should not just assume, as
I discussed in the first chapter, that victims of coercive control
and domestic abuse behave differently from any reasonable
person in similar circumstances.

> Gray: I do not even have an attitude ... I wish you could see
> I did not try to make you look bad, I am dressing like this to
> take the kids out. I do not dress like that when you come out.

Butler: The fucking way you made me look, you die you bitch, I'm raging you absolute bitch.

These texts are a good example of what we saw with Rohan and Sada. Butler is making Gray responsible for how he feels in public, how he thinks he is seen, and the behaviours not only of herself, but others. She is held answerable for anything that dents his ego or status:

Butler: Housework needs doing. The whole kitchen, the toilet, the walls, the floors, the bedrooms end of.

Gray: Yes okay.

Butler: Do the toilet upstairs then your room. We are separate and keep to it or I'll flip on you bitch.

Butler is giving orders for Gray to clean the house. Domestic abuse often focuses on stereotypically female roles and expectations, like domestic work, childcare and sexual reputation and behaviours. There is the threat of violence in this example if she does not do it, and do it to his satisfaction. And we know she was frequently attacked and injured.

Gray: It was nice and sexy and good, and then you nutted me like I was a bloke. I did what you said the second time. You made me drink more too.

Butler: One last chance if you get it wrong you walk the streets so think about it.

This text reveals possible sexual abuse: Gray was trying to act out a particular fantasy and Butler headbutted her in the face when she got it wrong. She also says that he made her drink too much. Encouraging, manipulating or forcing victims to take alcohol or illicit drugs is not unusual in coercive control. This can leave victims vulnerable, not only because of the effects on their health, but the effects on their demeanour: if neighbours or others, for instance, see them drunk or high, this will make them appear to be a bad parent. It also gives great control over their actions. I have seen deaths where there has been evidence that the victim was forced to ingest drugs or alcohol.

Sada also talked of Rohan's sexual behaviours in her diaries. She talked of having to act out sexual fantasies, which upset her, especially when she was recovering from giving birth.

In the following texts Gray is in hospital and very ill. She cannot leave the hospital to come home and look after the children. Butler is in a rage about this: he does not want to look after the children. He has no care for her suffering, and there is no sympathy or empathy.

Gray: I'm in hospital. I am Heartbroken and destroyed by you. I've had half an hours' sleep in two days. I have more swelling and my jaw is not opening. The infection has spread onto my face. I'm on drips. I can't swallow, I have a swollen airway.

Butler: You will never ever get away with this. Leaving the kids on me. So again you'll not be returning home. What a mother. My God I'm glad cos you'll never do it again. Goodbye you are a disgrace and I hope you know it's over now. You are alone.

Butler: If one day you let me down again. If the list is not done or there's a day where the diary is not written I'm moving the house about for good. This will end very very badly for you, but you don't care, that's why you don't learn, if your mother acts up once, or you talk to me funny once, I'm going to hit you so hard. Either show me u can be what I want or you'll see a devastating response.

Butler has threatened to attack Gray if her mother 'acts up'. He is again making her responsible for the behaviour of others.

Also, he's talking about the daily routines Gray must observe. There are lists to follow and Gray must keep a diary that he has access to. Routines and rituals are being used. Those diaries, where Gray may tell of a perfect relationship and how wonderful Butler is, will serve him in the future if she ever leaves him. They will be evidence he can use in any court hearings or other battles he wants to win. They will undermine any accusations of abuse she might make. Some controlling people have said that they deliberately maintained false social media pages just to ensure their relationships looked 'perfect'.

The only diaries of any truth or significance in cases of coercive control are those the controlling person has no access to or knowledge of. In Sada's case there was such a diary – the diary I read. Butler quite probably thought that text messages between him and Gray, once deleted, could never be retrieved. He was wrong; I was reading them.

The day Butler won his battle to get Ellie back into his custody and his control was the day that Gray was shown the extent of his power. His arrogance was fed and he believed himself unbeatable. More importantly, a message was sent to Ellie and Gray that he was stronger than the system, the police and the courts. If you are afraid, the police and the courts may be your only escape route, and in this case that had been completely cut off to Gray. When he assaulted Ellie again and the little girl died, Gray may have been a terrified woman, but she was also a woman who did not believe that the police, the courts and social services could beat her abuser.

Throughout the trial Gray spoke up for Butler, and everyone treated her like the worst mother imaginable. Many said that she should have protected Ellie. Ironically, at least in some part, she may have believed she had been.

The criminal justice system further complicated matters in this case by making sure that Gray could never tell the truth about Butler. She was forced to sit next to him in the courtroom as a co-accused. Not only would his proximity have terrified her, she may have believed that he would beat the system a second time, and if he did, she would have to go back to him. If she had not been loyal in court, if she had breached the loyalty code, he could take his revenge and she was very aware of how dangerous his revenge could be. Butler's posturing and arrogance as he conducted his own defence, as everyone played his game, would have strengthened that chronic fear.

Protecting Gray from Butler is not about taking her side, or sympathising with her, it's about creating an environment where she is more likely to give and reveal evidence to convict him.

The subtle signs and codes that Gray associated with violence would have been invisible to others. The idea that she could ever have publicly told the truth is sadly only a remote possibility in these circumstances. Gray needed protection from Butler; she needed to be completely separated from him, and she needed confidence that he was going to lose. I do not say these things to defend Gray; I say them to show how coercive control works and how the system effectively helped Butler control his wife and children. The system did not reduce the fear; it increased it by showing it did not understand the threat. That courtroom was a place where Butler felt comfortable, even inspired. Gray was somewhere she did not want to be, doing something she did not want to do. That shifted the balance of power substantially into Butler's hands. As it turned out, Butler lost and both he and Gray were convicted.

Twice the system failed to respond effectively to coercive control. The evidence of coercive control was there, and it was there before Ellie was killed. In some ways the control and abuse meted out by Butler was not given importance, or it wasn't seen. Links were not made between his patterns of behaviour and his risk. This is why it's so important to understand what motivates coercive control and domestic abuse.

Trials don't teach us what to be concerned about, they present idealised and plausible narratives designed to win an adversarial battle. We need to look to other processes that are better designed to reveal what we need to know, to prevent future deaths.

Domestic Homicide Reviews

One of the more recent and important innovations is the Domestic Homicide Review (DHR). These are independent multi-agency reviews conducted after a sudden death that may have resulted from domestic abuse, violence or neglect. There is a statutory requirement for local authorities to hold these reviews and they have been in place since 13 April 2011 as part of the Domestic Violence, Crime and Victims Act of 2004. In the Home Office guidance for conducting these reviews, there is a requirement to see things from the victim's perspective and to make the families integral to the process. This gives those conducting a review more ability to explore what really happened without relying on defence narratives, what has been reported to the police, and the offender's position.

I have mentioned Frank Mullane and his charity AAFDA a few times in this book. This is because of their central role in introducing DHRs. The murders of Frank's sister Julia Pemberton and her son Will were the subject of the first unofficial Domestic Homicide Review in England and Wales: the Pemberton Review is publicly available and not anonymised. Reporting in 2008, five years after the murders, it paved the way for the reviews we have now and the knowledge available to the public and to professionals. Since their inception there have been some 800 reviews published.

I have chaired and authored some of these reviews, and each chair will have their own approach, to some extent. Some are more victim-focused than others, but without these reviews it would have been very difficult to conduct the research into the eight-stage timeline. These reviews provided, in many cases, crucial detail of the history of the relationship and the victim's experience of life with their killer. It is through the telling of these stories that the patterns and danger signs are revealed, patterns so strong that we can no longer deny them. We need to know the reality to be able to protect future victims and to reveal behaviours and patterns that we have hitherto perceived as low risk, if risky at all.

There is a swell of information becoming publicly available through better information gathering – partly via death reviews, and partly through individual projects, like Counting Dead Women. There have also been campaigns to increase sentencing powers and introduce new legislation, and to form codes of conduct for journalists. The eight-stage timeline is a part of this work, and all the work done by academics and researchers everywhere. We are changing the conversations: we have established that domestic abuse and homicide are not just about people arguing and losing their temper – there is a recognisable and forensic pattern, just as there is for serial killers and spree killers. It's time to consider controlling and abusive people a threat we should take very seriously.

Research suggests that when men tell stories of their offending, we are quick to empathise, and when women tell their stories of abuse, we are quick to make negative judgements. We make negative judgements routinely about victims, whatever demographic they are from. Although this may distance us from the crime and make us feel safer because we feel we wouldn't make the 'mistakes' a victim made, it is a false safety.

In my work with bereaved families, the saddest words I hear time and time again are 'I wish we'd known'. Knowledge is power.

EPILOGUE
A Final Word

My daughter met a controlling narcissist. She was very young and the isolation from her friends and family came quite quickly. Before my eyes I saw her transform from cheerful and motivated to clinically depressed, severely traumatised and demotivated. She lost all her friends, she left university, she lost her job and her accommodation. She argued with everyone when trying to defend him.

I cannot count the times she called me in the early hours, crying, and I would go and pick her up off the street in her night things, or injured, or just distraught. I remember driving fifty miles one night to get her. The police were called regularly and she was considered high risk for serious harm. This went on for two years.

Getting caught in the snare of coercive control can happen to anyone. I am sharing this story because it is important to show that I do not sit on high, dispensing advice as if I could never be touched. I was touched, and I found myself on the other side. Despite being a specialist in this area, I was personally at the centre of a case of escalating and high-risk abuse. It was an edifying experience. This was my daughter and I wanted to protect her; I wanted her to leave him; I wanted him punished – all those normal feelings any parent would have. But I knew enough about coercive control to realise that I could not expect those things to happen just because I wanted them to. This was more likely to be a long game.

During this period I had to reconfigure my relationship with my daughter: it was no longer simply one of parent–child, where I could tell her what to do. I needed to be consistent, reliable and trustworthy: the opposite of him. I had to be kind, strong and non-judgemental. I had to behave in a way I did not always feel, like when I was frustrated and angry, or when I wanted to cry. This was about using the remaining influence I had to manage my daughter's safety, and to provide an escape route when the time came. Sometimes it felt like I was clinging on by my fingertips, especially as I was the only one managing to hang on to her. It was not that other people did not care; they did care, but they'd become frustrated with their perceived lack of power to help and influence her, or stop him.

It is surprising how much influence can be maintained, subtly. Just like fear, influence works in mysterious ways. Just because someone does not leave an abuser when you want them to does not mean you have no influence. Influence will not be a paternalistic 'or else' proviso, it will be like an antibody attacking the abuser's malign control, reducing their power. I also became acutely aware that the only person who could absolutely guarantee my daughter's safety was the person abusing her. He could decide if or when he would hurt her. He could decide to stop, or not. It was entirely understandable that she focused on him and what he wanted.

The good news is that she is now out. Predictably, he tried to get her back, but she resisted – she wanted to resist. She has a new life, new growing confidence and new friends.

During those two years, her abuser was rarely confronted and he was largely unaware of the police interest: there seemed to be no consequences for him. He might have believed from this, much like Vincent and Devin, that there was tacit societal support for his behaviour. One example stands out from this time: I was sitting in my car with my daughter one day when she received a telephone call from him that was made from a police custody suite. He had been arrested on an unrelated matter and I could clearly hear the shouting and the threats. I could see the abject terror on my daughter's grey and tear-stained face. He was able to make an abusive and deeply threatening phone call from inside a custody suite in a police station. This showed the confidence he had – that authorities or others within earshot would not confront him or criticise him.

It would not take much for society to completely change the conversations and let these controlling people know that their behaviour is unacceptable. We all need to call this behaviour out. As I have found during my research, the danger is not confined. These people will be a threat to their partners and children, the families of their victims, their own families, their next victims, and anyone else who might get in the way. It is not a private matter, and it is not simply a police matter; it is in all our interests to stop giving abusers excuses and justifications for controlling and self-centred patterns. Identifying a controlling person is a huge step towards minimising the damage they might cause, but many of these people stay under the police radar. We must be careful that in our media, courts, politics and social lives we do not stand in solidarity with them at any level, no matter who they are. To do so just feeds them.

When the conversations start to change, the practices will change too. Things have already started to move forward. Coercive control is now a criminal offence in the UK. We understand so much more about its role in homicide, and people can more readily recognise it and its relevance in thinking about risk. Police officers, probation officers, psychologists, psychiatrists, social workers and other professionals are beginning to be better at identifying it. People, whoever they are, can approach services if they are controlled, stalked or abused and be more assured than ever of support, understanding and help.

Fortunately, not all perpetrators of coercive control go through all eight stages of the Homicide Timeline. It is the minority who will go on to kill someone, but there are enough that do to concern us. Most get to stage three, and then to stage four or five. Many then veer off at stage five and the whole process starts again for a different victim at stage one, or they reinstate the relationship and they and the victim go back to stage three. But getting to stage three is not good for the victims; their lives and those of any children involved are restricted and they are more often than not left anxious, stressed and traumatised, brutalised and injured.

The most positive and exciting feature of the Homicide Timeline is that it sets out quite starkly when things are not right and offers opportunities at every stage to stop the progression. I have seen situations brought to a halt at every stage – even on the cusp of stage eight. If we are determined and imaginative we can create interventions for each and every stage. Those who are living with or working with coercive control will be well placed to think of innovative strategies. Let us not forget that many of our professionals are also victims.

There is strong evidence emerging that a history of domestic violence or coercive control is indicated as a risk marker for all sorts of other offending. The manipulative behaviour is not always confined to just the intimate relationship.

One of the biggest barriers is a failure to see and a failure to believe. When we start seeing control as dangerous, when we change the conversations, or even have the conversations, that will be the real and powerful beginning of change. If we can describe domestic homicide as unacceptable and abhorrent, then we will stop defending it.

The eight-stage model is having an enormous impact: it gives us permission to overturn and challenge the old traditional myths. We have the power to change this.

A NOTE ON THE TYPE

The text of this book is set in Adobe Caslon, named after the English punch-cutter and type-founder William Caslon I (1692–1766). Caslon's rather old-fashioned types were modelled on seventeenth-century Dutch designs, but found wide acceptance throughout the English-speaking world for much of the eighteenth century until replaced by newer types towards the end of the century. Used in 1776 to print the Declaration of Independence, they were revived in the nineteenth century and have been popular ever since, particularly amongst fine printers. There are several digital versions, of which Carol Twombly's Adobe Caslon is one.